Braided

Woven Together by Tragedy,
Three Widows Learn the Beautiful
Side of Grief

Deb Rooney, Gina Pastore,
& Debbie Siciliani
with Dave Franco

Braided: Woven Together by Tragedy, Three Widows Learn the Beautiful Side of Grief
www.braidedbook.com

If you would like to contact Gina, Deb, or Debbie about speaking or other engagements, please email beautifulsideofgrief@gmail.com.

Contents

Preface

Each step that Debbie took was exploratory. Following the "Camp Widow This Way" sign through the hotel toward the ballroom where the group would meet felt odd, and carried a bit of "I don't know about this" and "I can't believe I'm here." Her maiden voyage out of the house since her husband lost control of his white truck, due to a patch of gravel along a stretch of highway in the California high desert, brought her 2,500 miles to Toronto, Canada, by herself, rather wishing she wasn't. But she was desperate to find something or someone to be the stopgap to the searing pain that had renewed itself in her heart every morning for the past 13 months.

As she approached the double doors displaying signage that welcomed widows and widowers with cheery colors and exclamation points, it all seemed like a bit of new paint on a broken and beaten car. Window dressing. The best they could do under the circumstances. Lemonade from lemons. *Am I really here?* she thought. She anticipated smiling faces on the other side, smiles that would have to be forced through their tragedy to appear. She would have to do the same back to them.

As she was about to reach for the door handles, a woman walked up in a hurry to let herself in the room. Before entering, she turned. "Can I help you?" she asked.

Debbie began to speak. "I'm here for—"

"Oh, wait, are you Debbie Siciliani?" the woman interrupted.

"Yes, I am."

"I'm Michele!"

Debbie looked at her blankly.

"Michele, from Camp Widow."

"Oh, hi, Michele, I—."

"I have someone here you have to meet!" she said with her eyes like saucers.

"Okay," Debbie said. "Who?"

Down the hall at the makeshift Camp Widow gift shop, which was nothing more than a gathering of six tables with books on joy after grief and Camp Widow shirts and hats, worked Deb Rooney, who, as one of the Camp Widow members, was volunteering her time.

Debbie turned the corner, saw Deb Rooney, and stopped. They just looked at each other.

"ARE YOU DEB ROONEY?" Debbie asked, her lip offering a slight quiver.

"YES."

"I'M DEBBIE SICILIANI."

The crying started before they reached each other. Debbie fell into Deb Rooney's embrace as if it offered sanctuary from the horrors she had been running from. They stood and sobbed and trembled with arms, and souls, wrapped tightly around each other, neither saying a word. Minutes passed and still the two women, who had never set eyes on each other, could not let go. And they hadn't even formally met yet. But it wasn't about that. It was about safety in their shared experience of the same—exact same—profound loss. "I've waited 13 months to find you," Debbie was able to whisper. Deb Rooney just continued to cry and sniffle.

After that weekend, before returning to California, Debbie logged onto Facebook and posted pics about what had happened. Three-thousand miles away, in Southern California, Gina Pastore had just logged on. Suddenly, she saw that Deb Rooney had been tagged by Debbie Siciliani.

Gina's mouth fell open. She leaned back in her chair. "Oh my God," she said as she looked again. There they were, Debbie and Deb, in the same photo taken . . . in Toronto. Only God could have orchestrated such a meeting. A bit of Gina's life as a young girl started to float through her mind, the day she heard God's voice.

Part 1
The Before

- Gina -

Into the Quiet

There is a reason why the average italian home is uncommonly loud. First, Italians like to cook and fancy themselves as experts, which mean there is usually the clamor of pots and pans throughout the home. They also tend to express every thought that comes into their minds, which, when you season with a little disagreement, add a pinch of passion, and with the temperature on high, it tends to bring the overall tenor of the household to a boil several times a day.

Italian homes are also usually Catholic, meaning babies are encouraged. "Go forth and multiply" is a command from the Bible that most Italians attempt with vigor.

These are some of the commonly found Italian traits that were very much in place at our home, where my parents, John and Ann Pignotti, raised me and my three siblings—only our knack for creating a loud abode did not stop there.

Upland, California, in the '60s and '70s was a small and sleepy town at the foot of the San Bernardino mountain range that mainly offered developments of single-family dwellings amid miles and miles of lemon groves. With essentially one main street, it meant that kids had very little to do but make friends and move in packs between each other's homes. And with so much cooking taking place between my parents, both talented in the kitchen, the Pignotti house became every kid's main stop. There was almost never a time when the house didn't have kids, pre-teen to teenage, running in and out, so much so that I couldn't leave my room without at least a robe. I never knew who I was going to run into, often people I had never seen before—like the time my brother, Johnny, brought over one of his baseball friends, who was making himself at home walking up and down our halls. For a quiet, shy, 11-year-old girl, to unexpectedly run into a handsome local baseball star was murder. "Hey, Frankie. That's my kid sister." I wanted to die.

But it wasn't merely my siblings who drew outsiders to our house. My dad, like the great undeveloped land all around Upland, was a wide-open man, attracting people with his inviting personality and hearty laugh. He had more friends than most men and welcomed pals over all the time. And why wouldn't they come? With food on the table and another beer in the fridge, time spent with gregarious John Pignotti was a hoot. And because my dad was a contractor, our house always had a steady flow of men he worked with: plumbers, electricians, guys who laid pipe, painters, cabinet makers—all the sub-contractors—who came to talk, laugh, argue, roll blue prints across the dinner table, and smack each other's shoulders. Dr. Merrell, our pediatrician and my dad's best pal, would stop by unannounced, so too would our family friends the Angelottis and Cardilinos. Mom really should have charged for what was going down on a daily basis. The time spent cleaning dishes alone, even with Dad's help—and he always helped—was a heavy cost. Even our mailman would stop by to get a bite and chat. Kids, cooking, contractors, characters, and carriers.

One of the things my dad would do when he came home was to throw his boots off, turn on the television at full volume, and watch the news. He had to keep it loud, he'd tell us, what with the phone ringing off the hook nonstop and each of us answering and calling down the halls to each other. "Johnny, phoooooone!" Of course, if sports were on, no one had a hope of watching a show they might have wanted, especially if the Dodgers were playing. Dad, the Tommy Lasorda of Upland, respected and sought-after baseball coach to our town's most talented youth, played the TV loud enough to broadcast the game to at least the next three homes down our street. Dad lived and died with the Dodgers; his blood ran Dodger blue. Even his speech was blue, especially when things weren't going so well for the Dodgers.

These were the days before remote control, but that didn't mean Dad got up to change the channels. He would bellow from his chair to us kids. "Ginaaaaaa! Marinaaaaaa! Nickeeeeee!" We would have to run down the hall to turn the dial for him. "Hey, I work hard all day," he would say when we complained. "You do my job and I'll change your channel."

Between the roar of the crowd on the TV, Vin Scully, my dad calling to his kids to be his remote control, plus Pavarotti's [Ital:] La Boheme blaring from the stereo to close out the evening, the noise coming out of our home was exhausting. Of course, it wasn't as if Mom didn't contribute. She had "the girls" over nearly every day, a small contingent of neighborhood laughers: housewives like Rosemary Johnson and Teresa Pene, whose brand of conversation was made up of playful complaining about kids, husbands, and maybe a few neighbors, over coffee cake, cigarettes, and Sinatra's "I Got You Under My Skin" on the stereo. And they never believed one another. I know this because they exclaimed it all the time: "I can't believe that!"

"Me neither."

"Can you believe that?!"

"I cannot believe that!" they'd say every couple minutes, then break into another round of giggles.

Meanwhile, phones rang, doorbells dinged, rock and roll played from the rooms, friends and teammates continued to walk the halls to the fridge, Mom and Dad argued, and the overloaded TV speakers buzzed. It may be why I so looked forward to 8 a.m. every morning when my dad would drop us off at St. Joseph's, the place where every Pignotti kid went to school. I would walk through the large double doors into morning mass wearing a navy blue and white uniform with a red sweater and a sense of excitement for the moments ahead. There in the quiet, candle-lit sanctuary I had a sense that it was God who was behind the hush that leaned softly against my ears and soul; He required reverence to know Him. Coming from my world, I seemed to need it. It caused my breathing to slow and deepen and my eyes to close. I felt good there. It stopped me; it seemed to stop everything. The whole tenor of the cavernous structure worked perfectly with my shy demeanor, giving me no pressure to be anything other than what I was. Quiet. I loved it.

Even nuns and nun life held some appeal to me: their commitment to God, their strong ways, their fearlessness to do something they believed God actually called them to, even if it meant looking really different from every other woman, and requiring life without the company of a husband. I liked and respected them, especially when a cool nun would come onto the scene, which sometimes happened. Two nuns, in particular, hold a special place in my heart.

Sister Leone was from Ireland. She was young, wore cute shoes, short skirts, lipstick, and allowed her hair to fall out from underneath her habit so that it could be seen along the sides of her face. It almost felt like I was seeing something I wasn't supposed to—a nun being herself despite all the rules. In turn, Sister Leone took a liking to me, perhaps seeing how doe-eyed I was whenever she was near. She made me the teacher's pet, and I was only too happy to oblige. Her rebellious streak helped me come out of my shell. I wanted to be like her.

The other nun was a religious studies teacher. Unlike Sister Leone, she was traditional in every way, except for one thing: she had an unusual take on prayer. "Prayer is a two-way street," she offered. "When you pray, sit quietly for a few minutes after you've poured your heart out to the Holy Spirit, and listen for His voice. Sometimes He won't talk. But sometimes He will."

"A two-way street," I said to myself, deeply intrigued by the idea that God would take the time to actually talk back to little ol' me.

On that Saturday, I was eager to give it a try. As I readied myself, I remembered she said the one key thing that let me know God would truly be in the moment: I needed to find a "quiet place" to hear from God. *Yes*, I thought, *God is in the quiet places.*

Of course, that didn't exist in my house.

And so, on a beautiful day, I got my beach blanket and escaped the chaos of my house for the backyard, where I spread the blanket out, climbed aboard, and laid there—looking to anyone who might see me as though I was attempting to get a little sun. Truth was, I was trying to get God to speak to me about something that had been brewing in my heart for a full two years.

I was 11 years old the first time I saw Johnny's baseball friend Frankie Pastore at our house, and for some reason I couldn't put my finger on, he entered my consciousness and stayed. At 11, it wasn't a boy-girl thing, with hormones and all that. There was just something about him I immediately liked, felt drawn to, and couldn't forget. Was it his smile? His way? His rather overconfident air? Like Sister Leone, he was a bright new version of something I had seen so many times before: the shiny penny in a sea of old dull ones. When I was 13, however, just two years later, he didn't just dazzle my eyes anymore. He had made his way into my heart and I couldn't shut it off. I would even corner Johnnie whenever I could to pepper him with questions about Frankie—what he was like, what kind of girl he liked dating.

"He's a cocky dude," I remember Johnny saying. "And he has a cannon for an arm. Class president, too." It all sounded wonderful to me.

And so, I laid on my beach blanket and began to talk to God about it, to pour my heart out and see if God might just do the unthinkable and respond to one more girl lying in the grass with a boy on her mind.

"Dear God," I said, "you know all about me and you are all-powerful, and you know how much I like that Frankie Pastore. Every time he comes over, there is just something about him. And I know I'm only 13, and he's 17, but I think I can fall in love with him. And so here's the thing, I want to marry him someday. But if I'm going to marry him, he'll have to love me back. So here is my prayer: that Frankie Pastore would fall in love with me, that we would get married, and that he would be loved by thousands."

I stopped. "He would be loved by thousands?" I asked myself. "Where did I get that?" I had to think about why those words formed themselves in my mind. Was it because he had a cocky, overconfident air about him that I was fearful people wouldn't like him?

As I laid there in the sun, I tried to quiet my thoughts. There was no sense in getting out of my loud house only to have my mind racing. That is when I heard a voice.

"I will give you these things. But Frank is going to die young," the voice said.

I sat up like a shot. "What?" I looked around my backyard with eyes wide open. Nobody was there. "What did I just hear?" I felt my heart thumping in my chest. "Was I supposed to hear that?"

The backyard, including birds and neighborhood dogs, seemed to turn silent.

"No, no, no. This can't be how this is supposed to go," I said, fighting off a bit of panic. And so I laid back down with the intent of giving it another try, figuring I must have done a poor job and said something to throw God off course. I waited a few moments to gather myself.

"Dear God," I started again, "I pray that Frankie Pastore would fall in love with me, that we would get married . . . and that he would be loved by thousands."

"Gina, I hear you," God said. "I'm going to grant your heart's desire. But Frank is going to die young. Now I have a question for you: Do you still want to marry him?"

Without hesitation, "Yes, Lord, I do."

- *Deb Rooney* -

As Perfect Storms Go

The internet dictionary offers this definition for "perfect storm": A particularly bad state of affairs, arising from a number of negative and unpredictable factors that simultaneously converge.

The dark clouds of a coming storm started gathering over my life about three years before I was born. That was when two 17-year-old kids from Delaware saw no reason for their love to wait for adults to approve it, got into a '49 Buick, and dashed across state lines, 1,000 miles, to Mississippi where the laws were lax and offered little roadblock to child lovers tying the knot. The year was 1957.

Two years after their successful getaway, I was born in Los Angeles, California. However, it seems as though that was the end to their success. Trouble started brewing between Mom and Dad, now just 19 years old. Looking back, it seems no way that wasn't going to happen.

Mom, beautiful and capable, never came to fully believe in her own self-worth and seemed debilitated by a weakness to see the truth of who she was. And so she remained insecure and unsure of her place in the world. My dad gave her no help. He was a charming extrovert with a devilishly handsome face who took to the pool halls and found good times, a social life, as well as employment—he sold paper products and pool supplies to the halls in and out of the area.

It meant Dad was gone—a lot. Like most little girls, he was my world, and every day he was away was a bit of a heartbreak for me— one, because I loved him so much, but two, because Mom just never seemed to come out of her emotional fog long enough to be a friend to me the way both of us may have wanted. She would often lie on her bed with the drapes closed. "I've got another headache," she would tell me. Looking back I wonder if that was true. Perhaps lying down with the curtains drawn was the only way she knew how to deal with what was really going on when Daddy was on "another trip."

By the time I was 11, their marriage had reached its impasse and they divorced. I lived with my mom, my younger sister, and my brother, but my dad lived out there, somewhere, away from me—which made me feel terribly empty. I missed him so much it hurt. I remember riding my bike singing Carol King's "So Far Away" to him: "Doesn't anybody stay in one place anymore? It would be so fine to see your face at my door." My heart ached so deeply for my dad that something similar to a longing developed within me. I knew he must've felt the same for me—he had to; I was his little girl. But when I asked if I could live with him, he said no. The rejection rocked me. I wanted to be with Daddy but Daddy didn't want to be with me? It didn't make sense. In turn, nothing in my life made sense.

That was storm number one.

Storm number two actually began rumbling one year earlier. I was walking alongside my mom as we entered a store and the store owner, who was standing nearby, gave me a long look. He bent a little at the waist to deliver a message. "Good heavens, young lady," he exclaimed with eyes ablaze. "You look like Liz Taylor!"

"Who's she?" I asked my mom.

"One of the most beautiful women in the world," she replied, "known for being a spectacularly beautiful young girl—like you." I noticed the other shoppers looking at me. I felt it take hold inside. I was special because I was beautiful. The man said so.

I left that day different than when I walked in. I looked at myself in the window as we passed and liked it. A bit of thunder could be heard in the distance.

Sometime later, we moved to Anaheim and I was suddenly a new student at a new school. Up to that point, I had made friends easily and had never given fitting-in a second thought. But now as the new kid, I was alone. It was something that needed fixing.

I was at recess one day as a sixth grader and saw a cute girl standing by herself near me. *Perfect*, I thought. *She's alone. I'm alone. I'll ask if she wants to do something.*

And so I walked up to her and gave it my best shot. As if I hadn't asked at all, she simply turned and walked away from me. I stood there by myself, shaken and embarrassed by the open space all around me, while she walked away, everyone played with friends, and my invitation to her still lingered in the air. I suppose there could have been quite a few reasons that she walked away. Perhaps she was being waved over by someone else. Perhaps she had to go to the bathroom and a newcomer didn't rate in importance at that moment. Maybe, with her mind far away, she just didn't realize I was talking to her. Whatever the case, for a girl teetering on an emotional ledge after being so soul-injured by her dad, it was devastating. I was profoundly ruined by the snub. I had been a nice girl up to that moment, easy and confident, but suddenly everything changed. I was going to make friends, but no longer on anybody else's terms. It would be on my terms. No more Goody Two-shoes. No more playing by the rules.

Storm number three.

There was a crowd out there who would want me, and the worse I wanted to act, the more they would like me. I had seen them before hanging out on the street corners by the school as I walked home—kids who were up to no good but found each other to be what their parents, their teachers, and their churches feared. It was an adrenaline rush just to think about it. Better yet, I had a secret weapon. Sure, I was rejected by my dad and nice girls, but I wouldn't be rejected forever. I could do bad with the best of them. I had what boys—all of them—wanted.

As I suspected, making friends by letting down all pretenses of being good was as easy as walking up to a group of ne'er-do-wells and asking for a light. I suddenly had friends all over the place. The girl who would become my best friend, Denise, was my perfect partner. She was just as cute and alluring as I was and together we operated a friendship largely based on conquest—the cast and capture of boys. Sex Ed taught that sex with multiple boys was dangerous but they didn't have a clue what they were talking about. When I got a boy to desire me, it gave me a sense of accomplishment, elevating me right past the gnawing pain in my heart. I was a somebody—powerful and sexy. I made boys beg. I was 14.

Drugs and drink fit perfectly in the lifestyle. We did tons of pot with the other self-ascribed losers we hung around with, and the I-don't-care-what-anybody-thinks lifestyle with gusto. I got drunk with three other girls after lifting my mom's Manischewitz from the fridge. We were caught laughing hysterically and rolling down a grassy embankment at school before a school function, making an absolute scene. We were all suspended.

Mom tried to get tough, but she gave up quickly. She knew she was outmatched. I was on a tear.

I took a job at the donut shop in the Sears & Roebuck at the Orange Mall and found it to be rather perfect for me; I was like a kid at the fair. On my breaks I lifted jewelry by merely sticking it in my pocket, I stole clothes by taking a piece of merchandise into the dressing room and putting it on under my clothes, and I flirted with cute boys who seemed to be everywhere. Even the hot insurance salesman at the State Farm kiosk became a target. He was 25, nine years my senior, but it didn't stop me. The older the boy, the greater the accomplishment, the higher the high when I could tell Denise all about what we did. Conquests were fun. Telling about conquests was euphoric.

In my sophomore year of high school, a local hair dresser came and did a presentation to the girls. He was really cute. I made my move on him by going to him for my hair. But he wasn't like other boys; he was a tad smarter. He extracted from me my age and kept the relationship purely professional—until the day I turned 18. I ended up moving in with him.

I lived with Ross, the hairdresser, for two years. We were awful for each other. We were each other's green light for doing more drugs— mostly cocaine—and falling ever deeper into that lifestyle. We were productive during the day, holding down jobs and even getting promoted, but it was getting clearer as time passed that we were partiers before anything else—hard, hard partiers.

One day there was a knock on the door of our apartment. I walked to the living room to see my dad there with a serious look on his face. "Come out here, would you?" he said. "Can we go for a walk?" It didn't take long to realize that Dad was not there for a visit. He was there for something far more serious.

"You see what you're doing, right?" he said. "You see what you're doing? Is this really what you want?" Had those words come from an upstanding man, respected in the community, I might have shrugged them off—what could he know? But it was from my dad, a pot-smoking carouser. He knew the drug life and thought I was in trouble, that I had taken it too far. He had even traveled all the way to Corona del Mar. You don't do that unless you need to save somebody.

We were outside and it was daytime, and there was something about the harsh sun that seemed to heighten my ability to see what was going on in my life, who I really was. And I did not like it. When I went in and looked in the mirror, my skin looked bad. My eyes had lost a little life. Thoughts of how many times I had woken up after bingeing cocaine the night before and had no idea how I got myself home floated through my mind. I was living dangerously, going nowhere, doing the same things I had been doing for too many years. Mine was a paper-thin life, predicated on earning enough money to get high, laughing with my regular coked-up crowd, going to bed later than I should, pulling myself up at 6:30 a.m. to clear away the night before so I could perform on the job, and then doing it all over again. I was 21. I felt 31.

The perfect storm had merged into a hurricane.

Not long after that Ross and I parted ways. I looked to my co-workers at Wild West Store, a clothes retailer, to be my companions a little more than I had in the past, to fill in the gap now that Ross and the people I ran with had somewhat dispersed. Yes, I was using them, but that was normal for me. Being completely self-serving was my regular thing.

To celebrate a birthday, we decided we would go to the Cowboy, a country western dance place made in the image of Gilly's in the wake of the *Urban Cowboy* craze in 1981. I was dancing with Ted, a friend from Wild West, trying to follow the tricky western dance steps, and was happy the lighting was rather dark; we mostly looked like fools stepping on each other's toes. All of a sudden, a person emerged in my periphery. He walked right up to Ted. "Can I cut in?" he asked.

Ted looked at me like he had no clue what was going on. Not knowing what to say, I didn't direct him one way or another. The guy, muscular and burly and with an air of confidence, just stood there like it never really was a question. He was going to dance now and he was going to dance with me.

Ted moved aside and that was the last I saw of him. I looked into the eyes of the cutter as I put my hand in his, and when he held it, it wasn't like someone taking my hand but someone taking me. I had never felt anything like it before.

- *Debbie* -
My Rapidly Receding Mother

My mother was a sunflower and everybody was the sun. She faced and opened up to everyone with a smile and outstretched arms. She was made of love, and if you ask anyone who knew her, her loving way is the first thing they will talk about; it was her most prominent characteristic. Dad seemed tough and overly strict, but that might have been the result of being in such sharp contrast to my mom, who rushed in to tend to every need. Mom was a fierce protector, whether we suffered an injury, harsh treatment from a friend, or just needed a listening ear. Mom exuded kindness, nurturing, and caring and was a beautiful example of a strong woman of faith. She hugged the world away. I loved everything about her.

I was six years old when Dad came home to announce that a life-change was about to happen. He had been offered a job up north, and we were moving from our home in Highland Park, near Los Angeles, to a town in the Bay Area. We had to get packing. It was an exciting time.

The moving truck came and took away all of our belongings and would meet us in Concord, California, at a rental house; my parents didn't have time to find a home to buy on such short notice. A few months after moving into the rental house, my mom found her dream home: a small, quaint white house with French doors and a huge almond tree in the front yard. She was so excited.

The day came to move into our new home, but this time my parents and three older siblings had to do all of the moving themselves, as the new company my dad worked for had already paid for the initial move from southern to Northern California. When the move was completed and everybody was good and tired, my mom, bushed as she was, laid down, holding her back, and saying she had never felt so fatigued in her life.

Much to our surprise, a couple of days passed and she still hadn't gotten up off the couch. When it started to cause some concern, my dad took her to the doctor, who sent her home with a few pills and an order for continued rest. Many days went by and she still hardly moved; the pain in her back worsened. Back to the doctor she went, only to be sent home again with the same orders.

I was alongside her on the couch one afternoon as she was on the phone trying to find a tutor for me after I managed to flunk the first grade. She hung up the phone, put her hands on her chest, one over the other, and weakly called out to my older brother, "Steve, come here, honey."

When Steve arrived at her side, she gave a very soft but direct order, which was not like her at all: "You have to take me to the doctor. Right now."

Twenty-one days later, Mom passed away from Choriocarcinoma, a cancer that started in her uterus when a just-formed baby died in her womb but went undetected and was never expelled. By the time the doctors performed exploratory surgery, they found golf-ball-sized tumors throughout her body, especially in her lungs. She never stood a chance.

In the days leading up to her death, her cheeks started to show a little color. The positive trend prompted my dad and Steve to check on the construction site where they had both been working. On their way home, Dad began proclaiming to Steve, "I know God's going to heal her."

In the same instant, my brother felt a strong sense from outside of himself to address Dad's state of mind. "Dad, she might not make it. You need to prepare yourself if Mom doesn't survive."

"Don't say that, son!"

At that moment they turned the corner toward our house and saw parked cars in our driveway and on the street, including the car of our pastor, who had come looking for Dad. When Dad and Steve arrived, Dad saw the look of deep sympathy in the pastor's eyes. He went to the bedroom and came undone, slamming his fist against the bed like he was trying to punch a hole through it. "She can't be dead! Please, God, she can't be dead!"

I was sitting on the lap of my aunt. The louder Dad yelled, the closer she held me.

Dad's next task was to gather himself long enough to give the news to us kids, especially to me who would have the hardest time understanding. In the following days, my dad flooded my mind with Jesus, our loving heavenly Father, and the idea that Mom was in heaven with God and the angels. He and Mom were fervent Christians and attended Calvary Chapel each Sunday without missing. He spoke relentlessly about the unconditional love of Jesus and all that He did for us. In turn, it made me yearn to accept Jesus. That is when my dad led me in prayer and I received Christ. It was a miraculous moment, made even more miraculous when, as an adult, I would find out a little more about my father's frame of mind at the time of my mother's passing.

In the meantime, I had a mother to mourn, but it never happened. During the 21 days that my mom laid in bed at the hospital, I was not allowed to visit her; she was undergoing urgent radiation treatments that wreaked havoc on her body and Dad didn't want me to see her in that state. It had burned away the glow of life in her eyes and made her skin wilt and turn ashen.

I carried with me a distinct memory of being on her lap, arms around me, with tubes coming out of her everywhere. I would learn later, it was only a dream or vision—the imagination of a little girl who loved and missed her mommy.

I also was not allowed to go to the funeral. My dad didn't think I would fare well to witness so much pain and sadness, especially from him—he wanted to exude strength for me. In the days ahead, he took me to her gravesite to allow me to say goodbye. He must have believed that whatever went on there that afternoon was something he could endure while I grieved. But as I exploded into wailing, he came apart too, then was mortified that he had let me see too much. How could I come to him for strength, he feared, if I witnessed him destroyed and crying on the ground under a tree?

And so he never took me back. He continued to return to the cemetery every day, but as for me, Mom, once buried, had simply gone away.

In the coming months, Dad married Glynnis, a woman from San

Bernardino County, in the desert of Southern California. We moved to Claremont together with her and her four kids and started going to a new school. Suddenly my mind was occupied with getting used to a new life. But new sisters and classmates were not the only things on my mind. I was quietly dealing with a rare condition that brought early onset puberty, and had nobody to tell about it. I was now seven years old and horrified by my ridiculously early developing breasts and everything that went with it. Overweight and lumpy, I spent every moment trying to cover my body. It was a nightmare—endlessly emotionally draining. Just as terrible, I had extreme reading problems and was lost at all times during class, thus my poor performance in the first grade. All I wanted was to curl into a ball and die, never to be seen. Yet I was the largest, most eye-catching kid in the class. Perhaps worst of all, when my dad would ship me to Sacramento to spend time with my grandfather, I would end up becoming a playground for him. Inappropriate touching tore away at my soul.

In just two short years, Mom quickly receded into the past. She was not talked about and rarely mentioned. It seemed that when the casket closed, the book on her life closed too. I would often lie in bed and wonder how in the world we got here. How did Dad even find my new stepmother when she lived so far away?

There is an answer. Before we left for Concord, my dad was working a construction job across the street from where Glynnis lived in the Inland Empire, and a conversation turned into an attraction that led to more conversations, and then, and then. When my mom figured out something was going on, Dad confessed to an affair. That is why Mom took the bull by the horns. To try to save their marriage, she demanded a new life for the both of them and they started attending Calvary Chapel with urgency. It is also why my dad was so fervent about God at the time of Mom's death. It is a sordid part of our story, and yet, had it not happened, my dad never would have led me to Jesus. "All things work together for good."

Walking home from school with my new sisters one day, just seven months after we were made into a family, we turned the corner to find moving trucks outside our newly built home. Dad and Glynnis found the marriage could not continue. In a moment, my new sisters were no longer my sisters. I said goodbye, got in the truck, and drove off to get ice cream with my dad. Just like that, it was over.

A lovely woman named Carol came into my dad's life and within one year they were married. Carol and her five kids moved in, making us a home of 11. I would have to get used to a new family all over again, and so I jumped in trying to ingratiate myself to my new brothers and sister. One year later, Carol and Dad separated and divorced. Once again I was saying goodbye to people I thought I was supposed to love, and would love me, for the rest of my life. And once again, over ice cream Dad told me everything about how our lives were going to change.

Roxy was a young woman who took a liking to my dad when she saw him at a pool hall and asked him to dance. They were married only one month after my dad's divorce was final, and the revolving door of new moms and brothers and sisters started all over again. It had only been six years since my mom's death yet it seemed like three lifetimes ago.

The jarring back and forth of the life we led created chaos in my heart. I was as settled as driftwood in the tide. Nothing had permanence in my life and I longed for someone to come along and hold me, to let me know I meant everything for all time. Of course, for a young woman, especially one who had been rewired by a grandfather's perversions, opportunities for that tended to emerge in ways that one can grow up not feeling very proud of. It started in the sixth grade and continued on and off into college—me, trying to scratch an itch that just wouldn't go away. I felt abandoned and insecure, and every time I thought of my mother it would disturb me that it had been so long since the last time I had thought of her. She was so distant I hardly remembered her; her face and touch were fading like a photo in the sun. It was starting to feel like she never existed.

When I was 23, my cousin wanted to set me up on a blind date. I had just gotten out of a spectacularly dysfunctional relationship, fraught with physical and emotional abuse. The last thing I wanted to deal with was another man. But to quiet my very persistent cousin, I agreed. Her husband worked for my date, Jim Siciliani, who worked in a family business, Woodbridge Glass. The word on him was that he was very nice. Whatever. They're all nice until you get to know them.

As we walked into the company showroom where we would meet, Jim was right there behind a reception area. I remember his smile capturing my heart for a moment. We were introduced and within a couple of minutes, he had the audacity to bring up the girl he had dated the night before, as if I would have any interest. I rolled my eyes. *What a loser,* I thought. *Get me out of here.*

I went to the bathroom to think over how I might make a getaway. Just then my cousin came storming in. "Debbie! Jim said he likes you and is really glad I brought you! He's excited to go out with you tonight!"

I really didn't see the point. Yes, he had one of the sweetest smiles I had ever seen, but whereas most guys last a couple of dates before the first warning flags appear, this one waved his as soon as I walked up. Nope. No. I don't want to go.

"Debbie! Did you hear me? He likes you."

And yet, there was that crazy cute smile.

As soon as I sat across from Jim at dinner, it was as if our eyes locked on. We had everything in common, it seemed. He had had cancer as a child, and I had dealt with cancer too, because of my mother, but Jim's brought on something that had never crossed my mind could happen to another person: early onset puberty. It left him freaked out and fearful to be seen.

Oh my God, I thought. *Who am I sitting with?* I stared into his eyes like the future was slowly coming into view. We just stared at each other like neither of us wanted to let go.

"I don't think there's any reason for us to be here," my cousin said with a laugh and look of amazement. It's the only thing I can recall about her and her husband that entire evening.

A couple of nights later, Jim picked me up for a date . . . in a limo. As I got in, he said something with a look in his eye I couldn't put my finger on—it was a combination of seriousness and embarrassment. "I have something to tell you."

"What is it?" I asked, expecting some very bad news.

"I'm a virgin."

Could God really be this good to a damaged girl like me?

Part 2
The Dream

- Gina -

My Place in the World

Last: Motivated by a nun, Gina escapes the clamor of her parents' home to go into the backyard to pray and listen to God speak in reply to her prayers. She prays about a boy, Frankie, who has captured her heart, and then she listens. And then God speaks.

Frank kissed me on the cheek as he walked past. "I love you, honey," he said. "Oh, tonight is Monday Night Football. Have dinner ready as soon as I get home from work?"

"Of course," I replied from my spot at the kitchen table as he walked toward the garage in the bright morning rays blasting through our kitchen windows. Frank loved Monday Night Football—never missed a game, and always felt the need to remind me about dinner even though I hadn't missed one in 34 years. But that was okay. He was cute like that.

"Okay, bye," he said with a wave.

"B'bye!" I heard the door shut to the garage and the garage door opener begin to do its lifting. I sat there for a moment waiting for the sounds of his leaving—the kickstarting of his motorcycle and the garage door closing behind him, when all of a sudden I heard the Holy Spirit speak to me.

"Get up and go tell him you love him."

It was such an odd, unexpected thing to hear. It made me stop. "He knows," I pushed back. I was a bit too lazy at the moment to part with my comfy chair and coffee.

"Get up and go tell him you love him," I heard again.

I rather begrudgingly walked outside to find him with his helmet on and sitting on his purring motorcycle. "Hey, honey, hold on a second," I called out.

"What is it?"

"Well, I love you and I want to kiss you goodbye," I said playfully.

Seemingly befuddled at the break in our everyday routine, Frank flipped up the visor to his helmet, exposing his handsome nose. I kissed it. "I love you."

"I know," he offered, as if to say, You think I don't know that? If there's anything I know, it's that. It was true. Sure, I did miss my opportunity to tell him earlier that morning, but I told him all the time because I loved him more than those three words seemed to be able to convey. I just always wanted him to know.

"I know you know," I said as I gave him a smile and stepped back to let him pass. With the flip of his visor, he roared down the canyon. I just stood there and watched and let my mind drift a little in the morning sun. I felt profoundly content—happy with my place in the world. I had exactly what I wanted: 34 years of being married to Frank Pastore, doing fun and important things together, with a family of grown children who I enjoyed endlessly and were giving me beautiful grandkids.

It was the dream come true, the one that my mom, had she had her way back in 1976, would have put a stop to. Of course, on paper she was right, logical and perfectly sound in her judgment and dislike of what was going on. Little did she know that part of my motivation to do the desperate, crazy thing Frank and I ultimately did do was because of her; she just wouldn't give it up—daily screaming at me that I was too young to be so serious. I couldn't take it anymore.

But truthfully, the entire relationship with Frank was partly her fault—my dad's too.

When Frank, after spending a year pitching in the Cincinnati Reds' farm system as a 19-year-old kid, just one year removed from high school, was driving to my house to see my dad, who he loved, and my brother, his best pal, I happened to be walking home from school in my St. Lucy's navy and white uniform. I had just turned the corner toward my house.

"Wow, Gina, is that you?" he called out from his convertible 280Z. I turned around and saw who it was.

"Hi, Frank," I managed to say like 300 watts hadn't just passed through my body. He just stared at me a moment as he drove one mile an hour. Suddenly he hit the gas and drove right to my house and ran inside.

I entered our home and saw him and my dad sitting down and having a talk. I nonchalantly walked past like I didn't care, but when I got to my bedroom I ran around at full speed putting on lip gloss, redoing my hair, and checking my look. Suddenly, I heard Frank call, "Hey, Gina, can you come out here?"

When I went out to the living room, my dad and Frank were catching up on Frank's baseball season. Much to my surprise, after Frank recognized that I had walked into the room, he turned to my dad. "Can I take Gina on her first date when she turns 15?" he asked. My dad seemed speechless for a moment, not at all expecting a question like that. He always said I couldn't date until I was 16, so I was pretty sure the next words out of his mouth would be "Sorry, no." But my fifteenth birthday was about a month away, and this was Frankie Pastore, a boy my dad loved and trusted. Maybe an exception might be considered?

Dad shifted in his chair. "I'll have to talk it over with Anna. We'll think about it." I gave off a reaction like, Sure, okay, whatever would be fine. But inside I was, DaddypuleeeeezletmegooutwithFrank!

About three weeks later, I was attending a St. Lucy's dance held at our outdoor amphitheater, which rests picturesquely at the foot of the nearby mountains. It was a beautiful evening with the moon casting deep shadows beneath the trees all around. I was standing with my longtime friend Mia, watching our classmates dance, when all of a sudden she pointed. "Oh my God! That's Frank Pastore! What's he doing here?"

I did my best to find the destination of Mia's pointed finger, to see if who she was looking at really was Frank. Sure enough, there he was, dancing with a junior cheerleader. "Hmm. I'll be darned," I said casually. "That is Frank." Inside, however, I was saying, Oh my God! That's Frank Pastore! What's he doing here?

We watched a moment. "He's so cute! And you have a crush on him, right?" Mia asked.

"He's a family friend. Maybe a little."

31

Just then I felt a tapping on my shoulder. It was Brett, the freshman brother of my brother Johnny's girlfriend. He was from Damien High, the local all-boys version of St. Lucy's all-girls Catholic school. My brother had told me about Brett, that he was tall and good looking and nice. Johnny thought we should meet at the dance, and I had completely forgotten. "You Gina? Johnny's sister?"

"Oh, yeah, hi," I said to Brett, a boy I had never laid eyes on before.

"Wanna dance?"

We walked out onto the floor and added ours to all the bouncing bodies and heads in every direction. With the most subtle of head movements that I integrated brilliantly into my dancing, I would peek over to catch glimpses of Frank. Was he having fun? Was she having fun? Were they an item? Could he have fallen for her in just the last three weeks?

Suddenly, "Taking Care of Business" came to an end, and Bill Withers's "Ain't No Sunshine" came through the speakers—an awkward, slowish mid-tempo tune.

Oh, great.

Everyone defaulted to the slow dance embrace and we did too— exactly what I didn't want to happen. I looked straight ahead and told myself to just try to get through it. I didn't want to see Frank in the arms of someone else, so I was on high alert not to let him enter my field of vision. It seemed to be working.

"And I know,

I know,

I know,

I know,

I know,

I know . . ."

All of a sudden, I heard, "Mind if I cut in?"

I looked up to see Frank standing there. My heart started to race. Gentleman that Brett was, he stepped aside and offered me to Frank, who looked at me, moved in, took my hand, and pulled me close.

Oh my God, am I dreaming right now?

Frank moved his face close to my ear as we danced. I got a chill. "I never heard from your dad," he whispered. "I still want to take you out for your first date. Still alright with you?"

"Of course," I said a little breathlessly.

We were able to be in each other's arms for one more dance before the clock struck 10 p.m. and the night came to a close. Frank said he'd talk to my dad again. Two days later, he did. Dad said he and my mom gave their consent. Frank could take me out on Thanksgiving, the night I turned 15.

As it just so happened, Frank had been invited to Thanksgiving dinner by Johnny, and so there we were, all of the Pignottis and Frank, sitting around the table for what felt like an awkwardly chaperoned pre-date dinner, Italy, circa 1927, with everyone painfully aware and watching—especially my mom, who seemed excited to the point of giddiness about the whole thing. I couldn't wait to get out of there.

That night Frank took me to a movie, where we held hands, and then to coffee, where we talked so easily it was like picking up from a previous conversation we never had. We both felt it. Our personalities mingled and intertwined with such ease and seamlessness. We were like one thought. "Man, you're easy to talk to," he said. "I wish you weren't so doggone young."

When he took me home, he gave me a long kiss in the car and then again on our doorstep. I couldn't tell if it was a beginning or an end. He would be leaving soon to go back to playing in the Reds' system in just a few days. "If I do come back to Upland next year," he said, "maybe we can go out again?"

"Sure, that would be great," I replied. Was this super-handsome hotshot baseball star with slews of girls chasing after him really going to remember me in one whole year?

One year later, after playing single A ball in Tampa, Frank came back and wasted no time coming over to see my dad to ask if he could take me out again. Dad said yes. Mom said yes. We went out. That was all it took. We were together, like Romeo-and-Juliet together—madly in love, where one stopped the other started. He was 20; I had just turned 16.

The community was abuzz at our scandalous relationship and couldn't get enough of it—the pro-baseball player and the sophomore in high school. My mom was feeling the heat we were giving off, and with one swing of my bedroom door she put a stake in the ground. "You're too young to be carrying on like this with a man!"

SLAM!

It burst open our relationship, and suddenly we were at war. I was

Frank's and nothing my overprotective mom could say was going to get me to accept any other kind of arrangement. And so we fought like two lions in a cage, turning our house into a detonation zone. We startled the neighbors and rattled the china. Dad couldn't stand it a minute longer and entered into the fray, screaming at both of us as we screamed at him and each other. Day after day turned into weeks and months of fighting that left the rest of the family shell shocked and as unseen as possible. But I was not going to relent, and Mom never backed down one inch. She was going to save me from all the awful decisions she was sure we were already making. "Boys that age are not just looking to hold hands, you know! I know what's going on! Boys just want one thing! Sex!"

"You don't know anything!"

SLAM!

Night after night we went at it. It was exhausting.

I was lamenting my mother to Frank one night on the phone. "I just want to get out of here, you know? I can't stand it one more day. She makes me so miserable." That's when he made one simple statement, a stream-of-consciousness utterance that was the beginning to an idea that turned into a plan that became a reality and changed our lives forever.

"Man," he said, "I wish we could just elope."

Our elopement, and all that took place to make it happen, has been well documented and the accounts can be found in two separate books, one written by Frank (*Shattered*) and the other written by me (*Picking Up the Shattered Pieces*). Suffice it to say, it's riveting reading, with detailed plans, hidden clothes, decoy plane tickets, cops and police detectives, chase scenes, two separate justices of the peace, two states, and one angry, angry father. In the end, I was the teen wife of a double A baseball player about to be called up to the big leagues. My life had just flipped upside down.

After Frank got the call and a big league contract, we were on top of the world. Desperately in love and feeling like we had won the lottery of life, we bought a condo in Cincinnati, a Cadillac and a Porsche, plus whatever else Frank thought would make me happy. He made me happy.

And so there we were, living high on the hog, stratosphere existence with Frank, the youngest player in MLB, growing into a bona fide star. As for me, I was his adoring wife in designer clothes hiding the fact that somehow, for all the excitement of our success and wealth, it never quite seemed to feel as good as I thought it should. I knew I wasn't crazy the day Frank came home and said something to me that had been knocking around his heart. "It's funny, babe," he offered thoughtfully and perhaps a little troubled. "None of this stuff feels like I expected. Shouldn't I feel happier?"

Maybe it will in time, I thought. I figured it had to.

Over the next few years, Frank continued to put up great numbers. The kid with the "cannon for an arm," as my brother put it all those years prior, was living up to his potential and it was a thrill to see. He told me that Johnny Bench warned him, "You're always only one pitch from humility." So far, that one pitch hadn't happened—not even close. Frank continued to win games and his star continued to rise.

But with a bit of irony, just five years into the league, Frank's heralded fastball rocketed off the bat of Dodger Steve Sax and crashed into the tip of Frank's elbow, effectively shattering it. Johnny Bench's words to Frank echoed loudly in both our ears.

The year that followed was tough for Frank. No longer was his star rising; he was relegated to the bench wearing a cast, a frown, and a deeply contemplative look on his face. Recovery time was downtime— long hours of waiting or rehabbing. It gave him great stretches of time to think and feel. The nagging sense that there had to be more to life than the occasional limelight and accumulation of wealth wouldn't leave him. His dissatisfaction grew. He lamented to me frequently. How could having it all fall so short?

When Frank divulged his feelings to the team chaplain, he was given two books to read: Evidence that Demands a Verdict, by Josh McDowell, and Mere Christianity, by C. S. Lewis. It was all that was needed. Worldly success always leads to disillusionment. Only Jesus fulfills the soul. Frank gave Jesus the keys to his heart and life.

"I just accepted Christ as my savior!" he said on the phone, more excited than I had ever heard him. "And you have to too!"

I did accept Jesus, but not until after I ran as fast as I could from anything too Jesus-y. I thought my husband was turning into a Jesus freak, and as a Catholic, I wanted nothing to do with it—I didn't need it. I had believed in Jesus and the Church my whole life and didn't feel I required anything else in order to be whole. But one day, after months of chasing me down, I relented and went with Frank to a Bible study held by one of his teammates and his wife, Tom and Susan Hume. I found myself sincerely enjoying it and my interest was piqued by the idea of a personal relationship with God through faith in His Son. Not much later, I gave my heart completely to Jesus. Frank and I not only had each other, but we also had a relationship with the living God. The joy and excitement were almost too much to bear.

Ultimately Frank never fully recovered from the injury, and with a short, unceremonious conversation with player-manager Pete Rose, he was released from the Reds. He played one year with the Minnesota Twins before it was all over. He was just 27 years old.

Of course, with God, bad news tends to not stay bad for long. We both looked forward to a post-baseball life of ministry, and God ultimately turned Frank's interest in Christian apologetics and presenting the gospel to audiences into a guest spot on a popular radio show in Los Angeles, which turned into an offer to have his own show. "The Frank Pastore Show" was an absolute hit on KKLA, winning the National Religious Broadcasters Show of the Year twice in Frank's nine-year radio career. For Frank's post-baseball life, he had really found his lane. As his wife, I did too.

And that is where I found myself that morning as Frank rode away and I could hear the roar of his motorcycle fade into the distance. He was on his way to another three broadcast hours of making the case why only Jesus can satisfy the soul. Everything else falls short.

How I loved my life and journey. My mom, with all her protestations in the early years, was just doing what any mom would do—what even I might do. I was so thankful to God.

The rest of that day, there was plenty on my to-do list, with people to call, clothes to get through the laundry, and errands to run. And so I got right to work. Later, at 4 p.m., I turned on Frank's show, which I did every day, and started preparing dinner. He was talking to a professor from a local Christian university about how the body and soul are two separate entities when he said, "You know I ride a motorcycle, right? At any moment I could get hit and be spread out all over the 210. But that's not me; that's just my body parts."

"I wish he wouldn't say things like that," I said aloud to myself.

At 7 o'clock, the show ended and I knew from him having done it so many times that his full commute, after wrapping up, sharing a few words with the producer, and walking down to the building's garage, was exactly one hour. He would be home by 8 p.m.

When 8 o'clock came, I flipped on the game and put the food on the table so that his transition from the garage to his fork would be one easy motion. I loved to make him happy. When 8:15 came around, I started to search my mind for what might have caused him to be unexpectedly late.

Traffic, I surmised. He must have run into traffic.

When 8:30 rolled around, I started to get a pit in my stomach. *He always calls when he's going to be late*, I thought. I checked my phone. I looked at the TV with the game playing away on it, the one he didn't want to miss.

At 8:45, I called his producer, J.J.

"Hello?"

"Hi, J.J. It's Gina. Did Frank leave on time?"

"Yeah. Sure did. Haven't heard from him?"

"No."

"That's weird."

"Yes."

He took a moment to think. "Hmm. Let me go down to the garage and have a look."

"Thank you."

After a few minutes, the phone rang. "Hi, Gina, hey, uh, yeah, there's been a crash on the 210. I'm sure it's nothing but here's the number to the CHP. You may want to give them a call."

I took down the number with shaking fingers. I hung up and clicked on again. I started to dial but with each press of a button, I felt myself sinking, sinking, sinking.

Interruption of a Wedding Plan

Last: Debbie's father's leaving and subsequent divorce from her mother, including rejecting her when she asked to live with him, hurts her deeply. After a girl she does not know snubs her, there is something about the embarrassment that sends her over the edge. She pursues a rebellious life with abandon. When a handsome guy cuts in on a dance at the Cowboy, he looks like an answer to the problem of being her.

I was 21, seven years into my life as the sole driver of it, when Bill stepped up, looked me in the eyes, and conveyed, just by being who he was, that things were going to be different now. One might think— even I might think—I would push back against his take-charge way, but funny thing was, everything about him and his confident air was like a comfy chair after an exhausting climb up a hill on a cold, windy day. My body, my mind, and my inner turmoil came to a restful stop. I breathed deeply and sighed, as if Bill was a blanket I pulled over my chilled shoulders.

Bill had an electrical contracting business at just 26 and was already off to the races with it, making deals, growing his client list, drawing up plans for expansion. And he saw in me the love he had been waiting for, as well as his perfect partner for the future he saw. I was ready for the adventure. Wherever he was going, I was along for the ride 100 percent. When we got married a year and a half later, it occurred to me that Bill had never even proposed. We both simply jumped onto the same wavelength immediately, the kind that rushed toward marriage without the need to even have a conversation about it. Right from the start we were as sure as sure could be.

It was such a whirlwind of emotion and excitement that I never had a moment to look back at my life, like I can now, and see the trajectory of it: I was the wayward girl who couldn't be controlled by her mother, talked tough, loved recklessly, and traveled a dangerous, druggie path with abandon—and didn't actually like it. If I had, I would have never been so moved by Bill. The day he cut in on my dance at the Cowboy was the day he cut in on my lost-girl life.

Thank God.

Bill had been briefly married before, but it ended when his former wife revealed that she didn't want to have kids like he had assumed. He wanted a family and a stay-at-home wife to offer his children all the stability of an Ozzie and Harriet household. Without even asking myself whether I was the one to do it, I told him I wanted exactly what he wanted.

But when our first son, Patrick, came along, the domestication that was required of me wasn't exactly the easiest fit. Just a few years earlier, I was spending night after night snorting cocaine on a couch with my stoner friends until 2 a.m., and all of a sudden I was walking around the house with a baby in my arms, an apron around my waist, and recipes stuck to the fridge. I began to feel like I walked in on someone else's life. I wondered how I would fare in the role for the next 25 years and beyond. Tension between Bill and me began to appear for the first time.

But like an extraordinary bit of good timing, God seemed to ever so lightly ring a small bell in my heart during the pregnancy—a strange sense that the life inside me was much more than the common function of the female body. I could feel that something divine was taking place. It made me feel and think things I had never before.

There was also the time when Bill's sister, Kathy, and her husband, Bob, went in with us in the building of a cabin in Big Bear, California. On the way home down the mountain, their five-year-old little boy turned to me. "Do you know Jesus?" he asked.

Everybody chuckled at the cute words coming from a child. I laughed too. "Well, no, I don't," I replied.

"Oh, well, you should get to know Him," he said flatly. I smiled and looked out the window. I acted like it was just a passing adorable moment. But it got me thinking. Just then we hit the open road. It gave me plenty of spacious miles to ponder what had just happened and what my answer was to his simple question. And there it was again. God seemed to be ringing that small bell.

Soon after, I was talking to Denise, my old partner in crime, and she began to tell me about going to church, learning about Jesus, and how her life was changing. Neighbors began bringing up Jesus here and there, and I began to think, *What's going on?*

I was alone by a pool in Palm Springs one afternoon reading a book given to me by Denise—*Me? Obey Him? The Obedient Wife and God's Way of Happiness and Blessing in the Home*—when there, on the final pages, was a prayer that, were I to pray it, would let me know the Jesus everybody was talking about. I looked at the prayer just sitting there. Nobody was pushing me. There seemed to be no reason not to say the prayer, to "let Jesus in" as I had heard it said. Besides, God's nudging had developed into a fairly hearty dinging by then. And so I prayed.

The sky didn't part. Trumpets were not heard overhead. But I do remember a peculiar awareness in the coming days that indicated something in me had changed. Things I was hearing from the outside—coarse things said on TV and radio, even foul language made me uncomfortable—and this from a girl who effortlessly lived and partied with people whose language regularly peeled the paint from the walls.

In time, I began to follow what the book was exhorting me to do, which was submit to Bill—as much as I hated that word. Bill was not a Christian at the time, but after much talking to him about it, he sat down on the couch with a Bible one afternoon. When he was done, two hours later, he had given his heart to Jesus.

The excitement he had for his new life in Christ, as well as mine, and my new approach to marriage based on God's instruction found in the Bible, suddenly shot us into a life of unexpected joy with our Lord and each other. We had hit a new gear we felt so undeserving of. How could so much have fallen into our laps?

In the years ahead, we added two more boys to our family, Sean and Colin, and the adventures and home life Bill had always dreamed of began in earnest. We created an existence where baseball and hunting were the center of the universe. We traveled on weekends feasting on baseball games, the great outdoors, and the growth of our boys into strong, able, goodhearted young men. Bill coached the baseball teams and carried on at home like the captain of a great ship bound for success. The boys ate it up. He would storm around the house bellowing a chant about making it to the Little League World Series like an announcer calling the game: "We're here in Williamsport, Pennsylvania! We're here in Williamsport, Pennsylvania!" He would say it over and over and over and the boys would join in. And wouldn't you know it, we made it!

Bill coached the boys to win after win, and up the ranks they rose, all the way to Williamsport—an almost impossible feat for a local team from Yorba Linda, California. We were never so excited. We didn't capture the World Series title but got very close. The whole thing is emblematic of Bill's life. What he put his mind to, he tended to get. He was a force to be reckoned with.

But Bill also had another goal: to become a pilot and own his own plane. Our business required trips here and there, and as the boys grew older, they found themselves playing in tournaments farther and farther away. And as they grew in their interest and marksmanship, the hunter's lifestyle called. So Bill got his license and bought a plane. We followed the boys' teams as well as answered the call to the wild, traipsing through the woods nearly every weekend of the hunting season.

We were a family constantly on the go, and we enjoyed every moment of it. The boys were growing up so fast and turning into the kinds of people we had hoped. Patrick was the leader of the pack as the oldest, and his sweet, compliant way as a little boy hadn't changed as the years passed. He was still good to the bone and had hardly given us a moment's worth of trouble. He was handsome, a great student, a great athlete, particularly adept in baseball, becoming a big local star, and a winner at all he did. But best of all, for all his winning and the accolades he regularly received, he still had a humility about him that was rather remarkable. Aren't young jocks who excel supposed to have some bravado about it?

As such, Patrick seemed to always attract the girls, which brought a lovely young lady into his life. Erynn and Patrick fell deeply in love and stayed together through high school and college (he got a baseball scholarship to Pepperdine University) and married immediately after. I was so happy for Patrick's life together with Erynn. They gave us a beautiful grandson just two years later who grew to call Bill "Grandpa Airplane." Bill was thrilled. I was thrilled. What else could we have ever asked for?

But it was our second son Sean's engagement to a wonderful girl named Jana that put a bit of focus on a piece of land that we had purchased in Colorado, one with an old broken-down barn resting on it. In their eyes, with a little sprucing, a lonely barn displaying a rusty tin roof in the middle of a Colorado field was the perfect setting for a wedding reception. I totally agreed. Jana was a horse gal. How awesome would it be to give her a dream like that? Bill caught the vision and jumped at the chance to travel out there to do the renovations. He couldn't wait to bring his to-be daughter-in-law's fantasy into reality. Knowing him, it was going to be spectacular.

In January 2009, Bill, along with Patrick, who eagerly joined his dad in everything, flew to our property in Colorado for the third time, with many more to go. The wedding was still 10 months out but they were getting a good jump on all the work. It was another example of Bill's work ethic: being prepared and doing the job right. It was also an indication of just how much Bill and Patrick wanted to make it special for our entire family. Everyone was so excited, especially Patrick. How he wanted to give his little brother and bride a wedding reception worthy of a magazine cover.

On the following Saturday morning, the day Bill and Patrick were to fly home to Southern California, I got a call.

"Hey, honey," Bill said.

"Hi. What's up?"

"It's blowin' pretty good out there, right?"

I stepped to the window. The trees were in full flex. "Yeah, it's crazy windy."

"Yeah, the weather report is that it's going to stay like that for the rest of the day, so I think Patrick and I will just stay the night and fly back in the morning. It's supposed to die down by then. Good with you?"

"Yeah, sure. No problem."

"Okay. We'll be on our way by 9 a.m. Love you."

"Love you, too."

Click.

On Sunday morning I was in our office at the front of the house at about 10 a.m. I had been distracted from some paperwork that I didn't really feel like delving into by a chance to modify a recipe that I thought Bill, as a diabetic, might like. I was thinking he was such a trooper about his condition—never complaining about not being able to eat what everybody else did and still having to give himself shots every day—when I noticed a car drive into our driveway. As I looked closer, it was my sister, Jackie, and her husband, John.

My mind quickly absorbed two thoughts at the same time: *How nice to see them,* and *What are they doing here on a Sunday morning?*

I walked to the front door and opened it. I looked at Jackie and saw that as she got out of the car she stepped forward rather heavy-footed and slow. I smiled at her and then stopped. Her red eyes carried the full weight of an I-would-rather-die-than-be-here expression. I looked at them both tragically pulling themselves up the steps toward me. It gave me a moment to think.

Bill was in the air. Patrick was his co-pilot.

It was snowing in Colorado.

Jackie was here with John.

An emptiness came over me that made my limbs feel numb. I leaned hard against the door and clutched the handle.

Jackie sniffled. "Deb—"

Two Miracle Boys

Last: Debbie's mother is rarely ever talked about again after her death, and so she begins to act out, trying to find the love that seemed to fade away with her memory. Things are looking up when she meets a young man named Jim on a blind date set up by her cousin.

When the headaches became unbearable, and a bottle of aspirin—an entire bottle—didn't work to reduce the pain, it was clear that a trip to the eye doctor for Jim, back when he was 13 years old, was the next obvious step.

The ophthalmologist took a look in Jim's eyes and quickly walked out and told Mrs. Siciliani that he needed to be taken to the hospital immediately—his eyes were hemorrhaging from behind. Surgeons found a tumor in his brain, but they also found it to be inoperable. Jim was sent home to die. So resigned to the idea that their boy wasn't going to survive, his mom and dad sat Jim down and tried to hold it together long enough to find out what would be his one last request in life. "A cruise to Alaska" was his answer. And that is what they did. They essentially took him on a cruise to grant his dying wish before his slow deterioration and death, and to give their final goodbye. It breaks my heart to think what that must have been like to live through. Would any of their smiles have been real?

But in a last-ditch effort to save his life, doctors made him undergo

26 rounds of radiation and filled him up with a serious steroid. The transformation to Jim's body due to the med was quick and disturbing. His face ballooned to twice its size and kept his arms and legs skinny. To him, that was the real death; nothing could compare to his metamorphosis into a monster for all his classmates to see and be horrified by. Worse yet, he started to gain great amounts of weight. A simple walk down the school hall was a gauntlet of stares and comments. Mirrors and glass windows were avoided at all cost.

Of course, when he ultimately survived the cancer, he was branded a miracle boy, especially by his mother. After a chance meeting with a plastic surgeon at a showing of Star Wars and the subsequent plastic surgery, his face and body returned to normal, and his new lease on life caused his demeanor to become particularly buoyant. Jim was lighter than air, smiling his way into everyone's heart and gaining a reputation for being the most good-humored, likeable, kindhearted person anybody ever knew. As the years passed, he maintained a childish delight in life and found kids and play irresistible. Never was there a time when Jim was in the presence of children that they didn't attack him like a big ol' bean bag, even as he got into his 20s and beyond. He loved and laughed through all of it. He was a clumsy and bruised smiley teddy bear.

It didn't take long after we started dating for Jim's name to become Jimbo to me (it had been to his brothers his whole life), a floppy-eared, lovable, huggable softy of a gentle giant, who grew a mind-blowing 11 inches in one year as a kid. I adored him—partly because he was just so cuddly, but also because I felt so blessed to have somehow found my counterpart. The combination of my early onset puberty and subsequent hiding of my weight turned me into, as a way of coping, the most high-energy ray of sunshine anybody had ever seen. Perhaps if people could be overwhelmed by how loud and loving I was, they wouldn't notice how overweight I was.

And so I loved broadly and aggressively, endearing many people to me and maybe scaring away a few. But as an oddball, I knew I was in need of another oddball to complete me. And then came Jimbo. It seemed impossible that we could find each other. But there we suddenly were, married and together forever. I was so happy. Only a loving God could have made it happen.

Of course, there were some complications, and one of them started to show up immediately in our marriage, as in, our honeymoon night. The damage to Jimbo's body as a result of the radiation left him depleted of testosterone. The result was hardly a glance at me in the way a bride hopes. It wasn't so much that he wanted to ravish me and couldn't; it just never even crossed his mind. It certainly crossed mine.

In the following years, injections of testosterone gave him back his sexual desire, but the radiation trauma had also left him without sperm. We were not going to be able to have kids of our own.

That was okay. It really was. I had been given my miracle man, and if that was all I was to receive from God, it was enough. And yet, He wasn't done blessing us. Medication for just such a condition worked perfectly with Jimbo's body when it wasn't a sure thing, and suddenly we were pregnant with a little boy.

Our little Nicholas was born on January 9, 1997, and I was a wife and a mother to two miracle boys who should have never been in my life—husband and son. But according to God's great love, they were.

In time, we added two more boys and a girl, and I wondered if we had the most fun, affectionate, and loving family of all time. Their intrepid adventurist father did everything to bring his kids joy, risking that they would grow up into self-centered brats. But they didn't. Somehow they seemed to know that with each other we were riding an extraordinary wave of blessing, lucky to have happened upon each other's lives. It was the most remarkable thing I had ever seen. Love and appreciation were all around.

Yet, every diamond shows cracks. And for us, there were two. Jimbo's lovable ditz demeanor began to increase to the point where it started to raise some eyebrows—and not just mine. Our kids and our friends started to take me aside. "So what's going on with him?" they'd ask. His clumsiness and awkwardness seemed to make appearances daily and at all the wrong times. With a smile and a laugh, he would be unable to remember the three things I would have just told him to go to the store to get. He would miss appointments that I had told him about just 30 minutes earlier. He began to forget the names of people we knew well, like our very best friends. He would say things he had just told me a few days before, and again a few days before that. He would turn uncharacteristically grouchy for seemingly no reason. Stopped at a stoplight, I would be looking down at my phone while sitting in the passenger seat and suddenly be startled by honks. Looking up, the lights would be green and the cars would be gone but Jimbo would be asleep with his foot on the brake.

I took him in to be evaluated for Alzheimer's disease only to find out the effects of his 26 rounds of radiation all those years prior were still breathing fire throughout his body and would continue to do so. It was actively taking him from us, burning away his mind and body cell by cell more than 30 years later. It didn't help that the radiation had been targeted on his brain right alongside his sleep center. We were losing him.

To make matters worse, a rift started between Jimbo and his brothers over his role at the company. The tragedy was that his parents and all the brothers and their wives loved being together. They all worked together, except the wives, 10 hours a day and we still went out to dinner, all of us, three to four times a week until we had children. They all loved each other so much. Hurting him was the last thing anybody wanted to do. But as Jimbo began to show more and more that he was not up to any of the jobs at the company suitable for the owner's sons, he was given an inconsequential responsibility in the back of the building that would require being at the office at 5 a.m. I know the brothers hated having to do it to him.

"They don't know what to do with me," he said, falling into terrible weeping after a major blow-out with a brother. The whole ordeal ruined him, cutting his confidence off at the knees. He sensed he was slipping away from himself and all of us. He knew he was lovable; he just wasn't useful. Sadly, he was right.

It was awful to see.

In the meantime, our kids were the center of his world, retreating to them so he could be himself and receive all the love and affirmation a man could want. And they gave it to him—especially Nick, who loved his father like a puppy loves his master. Ever since he was a baby, Nick could never get enough of Jimbo. Life had everything to do with his dad and little to do with me.

Our other kids gave me lots of love and easily showed their affection for me, sharing nearly every part of their lives. But not Nick. I would tell myself that he would change one day because I knew what kind of mother I was: interested, kind, loving, long-suffering, and I knew when to back off and give some space. Yet, as much as I tried, I simply couldn't get through to him. Years passed and he simply never saw a friend in me. He might hug me at the appropriate times, but I couldn't get him to let me into this thoughts and experiences, to give me a glimpse of who he was and what he wanted. Was it something I said years ago that he misinterpreted, something I did?

The remarkable thing is Nick could not have been a more beautiful soul. Accolades for our boy would come from everywhere: his teachers, his friends, his friends' parents, and his coaches. Nick's loving way, hysterical sense of humor, wisdom beyond his years, loyalty, and high emotional IQ were evident for all to see. But of all his outstanding traits, the one that seemed to be the most prevalent was his selflessness. Nick had a sixth sense for everybody else's needs. He was a friend to his friends, but he was also a kid who befriended the loners. He felt other people's pain.

As for me, however, when Nick would come home, he'd walk in, say hello, and walk right past. All my kids wanted to get my hugs and let me set out some leftovers or a cookie while they told me a story or two. Not Nick. If his dad walked in, he was suddenly different, of course. But if it was just me, it was always hi and 'bye.

"Maybe one day," I kept telling myself.

Nick was 16, a sophomore in high school, the evening he came home from the beach. The door slammed. I looked to see who it was. "Oh, hi, honey," I called out.

"Mom!" Nick said. "I had the best day!" He came over to me in the kitchen and sat down with a plop.

"You did? What happened?" Nick and his four other friends, the Fab Five, as they called themselves, had spent the day shooting a video, a group lip-synch to a song they all loved called "Battlescars," and it was so "freaking fun."

"Yeah, Evan is going to edit it together and it's going to be hysterical and I can't wait to show you. When it's done, I'm going to grab you to see it, okay?" My heart leapt.

As he went on talking excitedly, my mind was going in two directions. I had to take in everything he was saying, but I couldn't help but listen to my own voice shout from the rooftops, "My boy is sharing his life with me! He's really sharing his life with me!"

The next night, I was downstairs when I heard, "Mom, come here quick!" As I arrived upstairs, Nick was beside himself to show me the finished video sent by Evan. We had a wonderful time watching and laughing our heads off—of course everything gets even more hilarious when you are luxuriating in a moment you've waited a lifetime to experience. To him it was probably a lot of fun. To me it was one of the pinnacles of my life. I was walking 10 feet off the ground.

The next day, on Friday, Jimbo came home with a great idea. His brothers needed somebody to pick up a piece of equipment in Laughlin, Nevada, and Jimbo, spontaneous as he was, saw it as a chance for a guys' weekend with him, Nick, and Greg, our second oldest. Estimated time of departure: 6 p.m.

The boys and Jimbo got right to work packing, and I picked up munchies for the four-hour drive, all the while thinking how much I didn't like the plan. Jimbo wasn't good behind the wheel at night and his episodes of falling asleep while driving scared me to death.

As 6 p.m. approached and it was time to get in the truck, Nick made a quick stop in his little sister's room. He hugged Chelsie and told her he loved her. He had never done anything like that before, but they had been a little hot tempered with each other recently, and he wanted to make sure she knew how he felt. He knew she needed it.

"Can we pray before you go, please?" I called out when everybody had assembled in the driveway.

"Really?" Jimbo asked like, Are you kidding me?

"Please. Come on, everybody—in a circle," I insisted. We all took hands and, much to my surprise, my prayer-shy husband jumped right in and took the reins. He prayed for safety and a good time. It was great for him to do and I was glad to see it. But then came something I wasn't glad to see. As the boys jumped in the truck with me still standing at the front door, Jimbo closed the garden gate and began walking toward the truck.

"What?" I yelled out. "You didn't even kiss me goodbye? What if this is the last time I see you?"

"Come here," he said, beckoning me with the come-hither index finger.

"No."

"Come on, now."

I walked over and gave him a playful kiss. "See you when I get back," he said with a smile.

I walked to the other side, where Nick was rolling down his window. I stepped right up.

"You keep your dad awake, do you hear me?" I said. "Poke him, throw chips at him, just keep him awake."

"I will. Not to worry, Mom," Nick offered with a thumbs-up.

Too late.

Part 3
The Dream
Interrupted

God's Answer, and Mine

Last: Gina has just called Frank's producer to find out why Frank is so late coming home from the station when he had had such high interest in watching Monday Night Football. The producer calls Gina back to say that there has been a crash on the 210 and gives her the phone number to the California Highway Patrol. She calls.

It was approximately 7:30 p.m. when a midsized sedan quickly and inexplicably drifted two full lanes to the left and into the diamond lane, where motorcycles and cars with more than two people ride free from all the other freeway traffic. The driver claimed that she had been sideswiped by a red SUV, although no witnesses could recall seeing a red SUV at or near the scene. Frank was riding in the diamond lane when her car clipped the back of his bike, sending him into a desperate fight for control. Two witnesses recounted the gruesome scene—my husband flew into the center cement divider, hitting his head, then slid for several yards in a cloud of smoke, dust, and motorcycle parts spray. Hundreds of cars on the busy, chaotic Los Angeles freeway came to a screeching halt.

At that moment, I was stirring Frank's dinner in our kitchen, talking and laughing on the phone with my sister Marina while Frank laid on the 210 with people running to the scene and to his broken body. In the moments ahead, an ambulance would arrive and so too would a medivac helicopter when Frank was deemed too seriously shattered, too close to death for any conventional transport. Meanwhile I was turning on Monday Night Football and setting the table, maybe even singing as I often do. It's chilling to think of my husband's tragedy and what pain he must have been suffering lying on the freeway by himself while I was filling up his water glass.

Forty-five minutes after Frank was supposed to be home to watch the football game he was eager to see, I was on the phone, dialing the CHP to see if they knew anything about Frank.

"Yes, hi," I said with a quivering voice to the man answering the phone for the CHP. "I'm calling to find out if you have record of a Frank Pastore being in an accident tonight. It would have been on the 210."

"Let's see here. Wait a minute—you his wife?"

"Yes, Gina Pastore."

"Okay, let's see here. Hold on a minute. Okay, yes, I'm seeing here that there was a Frank Pastor in a crash. Let's see, he was resuscitated on the scene and then airlifted to USC medical center. Want the number?" He spoke with all the compassion of someone answering a customer's call to see if their dry cleaning was ready.

At once, I felt like I was having an out of body experience. I instantly felt dizzy and my limbs starting to shake. I clicked off the phone and stood in a deep stare.

When I called USC, I frantically told the woman who answered who I was and if she could please confirm that Frank was there. She then abruptly patched me to another location on a different floor where I would have to make the same request all over again, this time to a nurse. "You're Mrs. Pastore? Where are you?" she said like she was scolding a child. She demanded, "Why aren't you here?"

"Here" felt like an insult coming from her. He was there with her, away from me, in a hospital, when he should have been at home. What right did she have to have my Frank, and me not? "Nobody called me!" I shot back. I felt a chill come over my body. I suddenly started to shiver. I was going into shock. "Can you tell me—is he going to make it?"

"Can't say. We don't know yet," she replied.

I got off the phone, called my sister, and ran to the closet to get a jacket. I was suddenly freezing.

An hour and a half later, after construction on the 210 put an additional 45 excruciating minutes to our already long drive, my sister, Marina, her husband, Don, and I arrived at USC where we got lost among the different medical centers. Finally, after a security guard came to our aid and directed us to the brain and trauma center, we found parking in a distant lot and began hoofing it all the way, nearly a half mile to where Frank was. I was wearing Frank's heavy jacket, yet I was like an ice cube, a running, crying ice cube in sandals. I had the strangest sensation: as I ran, I was actually watching myself from above.

When we made it to Frank's floor, we were led to a waiting room. A neurosurgeon stepped in to give us the news: Frank had suffered a severe brain trauma, which had put him in a coma. He had broken legs, a broken shoulder, a compound fracture to one arm, and was on morphine. I had the distinct feeling that I was searching the edges of a nightmare, trying to find where the dream state ended, and the realization came to the fore that none of it was true. *This can't be*, I thought as I fell into a seat and felt Marina's arm around my shoulders. *It just can't be.*

When the time came that I could go into Frank's room, my heart pounded so violently it seemed impossible it couldn't be heard by others. The door opened. Frank was lying there looking . . . perfect. Eyes closed, his expressionless face appeared untouched. His entire head had only a small drainage tube coming from his beautiful bald skull. He was handsome, just like always, just like the boy I fell in love with.

I approached him slowly as if entering a new world I knew nothing about. I walked up to his bed. He appeared to be asleep, no different from any other time I'd catch him napping on a Sunday afternoon. I had one overwhelming thought—to jump on his bed, grab hold of him, and say, "Frank, let's get out of here. Come on, let's go, honey. We don't need to be in this place."

"When his head hit the divider," the doctor said, "it resulted in Shaken Baby Syndrome, where the inside of the brain gets jolted so badly blood vessels detach within the scull." I looked at my serene husband, my hero. I saw the equipment, heard the beeping machines. I could hear the talking and footsteps beyond the door. I felt grief start to come over me. I wasn't waking up. I couldn't find the end of the dream.

"Let's get out of here, honey," I could barely say as I held my tissue up to my mouth and ran my finger along the side of his body. I kissed the nose I had kissed that morning.

By 4:30 a.m., after six hours of being by his side, I suddenly had a strong sense that I wanted to go home. My home was Frank's home, where he smiled and laughed and loved me, and I wanted to enter into that environment again, to feel him. I couldn't hold him close in the hospital. And so, I wanted Frank's spirit to hold me as I stepped back into the home we had made together. There may have been nothing rational about it. But what did rationality have to do with anything now?

At about 5:30 a.m., I walked into the house after being dropped off. A little bit of dawn was peeking around the edges of morning. I turned off lights I had left on in the house when I ran out. Frank's place setting was still in front of the TV. I slowly walked down the hallway to my bathroom and turned on the faucet to the tub. I got in and laid in the water. Without thinking about it, something came from my lips, perhaps the one thing I knew for sure. I began singing:

You are my hiding place,
You always fill my heart
With songs of deliverance
Whenever I am afraid
I will trust in You
I will trust in You
Let the weak say
I am strong
In the strength of the Lord

Logically, there was likely no way Frank was going to survive brain trauma so massive. But my God said He is a God of miracles. That meant there was hope.

I laid in bed for two hours trying to sleep and didn't get close. Marina brought my mother to the house around 7:30 a.m. After we talked and cried and I told her everything I knew, we got in Marina's car and she dropped me off at the house of my close friend Veronica. Marina and Veronica had talked, and my sweet friend had offered to be the point person in arranging my comfort and safety during what lay ahead, and that I would never be alone.

Parking in the USC trauma center's distant lot once more, we began the long walk toward Frank. Suddenly, a couple of nurses called out to me from a distance as they walked past. "Mrs. Pastore, we heard about

Frank and we are praying."

"Oh, thank you so much," I replied.

Soon after, another staff person called out. "Oh, Mrs. Pastore, we are all really praying for Frank. Just awful what's happened."

"Yes, thank you," I said. In the time it took us to get to the front doors of the trauma center, we were stopped 12 times by people who had heard about Frank and were praying and wishing us well. It was such a surprise.

"Oh, Mrs. Pastore," the woman at the front desk said as we approached, "Frank is under an alias and we've doubled up on security."

"I'm sorry, can you say that again?" I said.

"Yes, there are tons of people trying to get in to see him, so we've doubled up on our security measures. He's registered under an alias."

What?! Who in the world is trying to get in to see my Frank?

"Ma'am," the nurse said, "we're also going to have to give you a code to give friends and family who you approve to come upstairs for a visit. Without the code, we are going to turn them away."

Codes and aliases and security measures? Who are all these people?

In time I learned that a good friend of mine had heard about Frank's accident and had posted it on Facebook. Within 24 hours it had spread like wildfire, and news of Frank Pastore, the popular Christian radio host on KKLA, who eloquently arbitrated the Intersection of Faith and Reason over the airwaves in Los Angeles, had reached around the world. I had no idea.

The baseball world was calling. Old Reds teammates like Tom Hume and Johnny Bench reached out. ESPN executives called. Athletes from outside baseball were calling. Prayer chains were started in far places like Africa and continued around the globe. Bible studies all over the United States and around the world were on their knees praying for Frank. He was just a local radio guy. How did he come to mean so much to so many? What was God up to?

Inside Frank's room, where nothing had changed from the day before, Frank looked like he was just waiting for me to take him home and finally eat the food I had made. "Seems like you've had quite an impact on a lot of people, honey," I said, my face red and wet. "If you only knew. Did you have any idea?"

At one point, I took a break and walked down the hall. A nurse was there. She gave me an I'm-so-sorry smile. "It's going to be a roller coaster, Mrs. Pastore," she said. I understood what she meant—there would be highs and lows. I had better hold on for what was coming. She had seen it all before—the emotional toll of the long stretches of despair. The brief flickers of hope. The endless waiting.

In the coming weeks, Frank's condition remained largely unchanged. We were all in a holding pattern to see if there might be improvement—some brain function, or better yet, that he might come out of his coma. Our kids, Frankie and Christina, and their spouses, kept vigil with me and took the whole tragedy extremely hard. We prayed together, cried together, stayed together, ate together and waited through the agonizingly long, long hours of silence.

Outside Frank's room, the vibe was different. Family, friends, and local pastors crowded the waiting room to pray and offer their support. So many people I didn't even know had food delivered to the hospital every day: sandwiches, chicken, casseroles, cakes, pies, even Italian catering flowed in. It was unbelievable—food and people were everywhere. We fed the nurses and staff and there was still plenty left over. Frank's bosses and work colleagues from the radio station showed up every day. One of them revealed the station hadn't posted Frank's final show as a podcast and then looked shocked when I responded with surprise. "Why didn't you post it?"

"Out of respect for you and the family," he answered. "Gina, it's the one where he talks about getting hit on the way home."

"You have to post it," I said to Terry, the GM. "You don't think God was guiding Frank to say what he did that night? God will use it to reach people." So they posted it. Frank's prophetic comment that he could be hit on the 210 on his way home caught on and was shared by hundreds of thousands of people all over the world.

Christina became my de facto PR person to handle all the calls; so many were coming in that my phone couldn't even hold a charge. The hospital had to set up a press room for me to take interviews from different news outlets and magazines. I was perfectly willing to grant the interviews. It had become abundantly clear that Frank, beyond my wildest dreams, was a very public person and the world needed his voice to continue. I gave updates and spoke on his behalf, reconfirming his belief that God, despite all that he was going through, was deeply loving and had a plan for every life, even his.

With all the people and prayer and food and provisions and media, as well as the well-wishes and thousands of letters, cards, hugs, and tears, God seemed to have turned the hospital into some kind of spiritual epicenter. One of the hospital staff walked over to me. "We have huge celebrities admitted to this medical center all the time, but I've never seen anything like this," he said. It was a shocking realization. I walked into Frank's room and looked at the sleeping boy who had caused so much outpouring of emotion. "God, what is happening? What are you doing?"

It was becoming clear God was using this tragedy for reasons well beyond my understanding.

Week three arrived and Frank's condition remained the same. People continued to come and pray and I felt the spiritual lift that so many prayers, scriptures, encouragements, and prophetic words of healing could offer. The broadcasters on Frank's station, Salem Broadcasting, kept the vigil, keeping their audiences apprised of Frank's condition—especially Big Wave Dave, one of Frank's good pals, who was a popular host on the FISH, a sister station to KKLA. He was relentless in bringing everything he talked about on the show back to Frank and the need for everyone to keep him in prayer. It was deeply touching and I was so grateful. I felt great amounts of hope. Even so, I reacted with urgency the moment one of the top neurologists in the world stopped me in the hall and made me an offer.

"I know it's hard to know what's going on, so I am happy to talk if you want to," he simply and kindly stated.

"Yes, please," I abruptly answered. "Do you think my husband is going to make it?"

He seemed caught off guard by my level of jump-in. "You seem very levelheaded, Mrs. Pastore," the doctor said. "So I'm going to tell you the truth. Every day that goes by that someone is in a coma and they don't wake up is a bad sign. I want you to remember that. I know the hoopla about your husband. And I know you are part of a praying community. I know there are a lot of people saying he's going to make it, and I am not saying that he isn't going to make it. I don't want to insult your faith. But it will take a miracle. I know you probably believe in miracles."

"Yes, I do."

He nodded slowly and soberly. "Well, that's what it will take."

At once I felt the pain of his words, and I was deeply grateful. If faith is like treading water in a pool, then the doctor's words were like finding the edge. I appreciated getting his medical opinion and respected it immensely. Even so, I still had hope.

I walked back to the room to see Frank, who was essentially brain dead and now fighting pneumonia and a fever. But his heart was strong. He could go on for years. What would come of all this?

After the third week, the hospital released Frank to a care facility of my choice, explaining there was nothing else that could be done for him. My first reaction to the word "nothing" was panic. But as the sober moments set in, I also understood.

In the care facility near our house, I watched with deep concern that Frank wouldn't suffer too much with how sick he had gotten. There was much less hoopla now that I had disallowed the masses to follow us to Upland. Still there were signs of God moving—a lovely Christian nurse wrote Bible verses on pieces of paper and attached them to the wall above his head.

Oh Lord, please move through your Word.

One afternoon, four weeks to the day of the crash, Frank seemed to be resting easy when Big Wave Dave came by. Dave was sitting near and doing his best to have a razz-filled conversation, something they did all the time, with his unresponsive friend, when it occurred to me that bills and other things that needed tending had been neglected for too long. I decided to rush home and get to work. If I was quick about it, I could get back within two hours.

I was buried in paper at my desk in my office when my phone rang. "Mrs. Pastore," said the care facility administrator. "Can you come back right away?"

"Why?" I said feeling my heart drop into my stomach.

"I can't tell you that. Can you just come back?"

As I parked my car in the facility lot, my feet felt numb as I began moving them out of the car. When I tried to stand, I could barely do it. I gathered myself and walked slowly to the front doors. My mind started to blur. The security guard saw me. "Go right to your husband's room, Mrs. Pastore," he said kindly and knowingly, like ushering me toward something he knew was the one thing I wanted least in life.

I turned the corner to walk the long hallway and I could see the administrator there in front of Frank's room with her head down. I knew why.

When I got to her, she pulled me close and held me tightly. "He's gone," she said tearfully. I felt my legs give out and suddenly my full weight was in her arms. I let out a terrible, guttural howl as if I had been saving any wailing for this moment. It came from somewhere so deep it no longer carried the characteristics of my voice. An uncharted part of my soul had broken out.

When I could gather myself enough to formulate words, I said, "I was just here and I left!"

"Gina, no. Your pastor was here. Frank wasn't alone."

Just then our pastor, David Rosales, approached to take me in his arms. "Gina, Gina, listen to me. I told him, 'Frank, either go home to Gina or go home to Jesus.' And as soon as I did, his monitor went off. Frank wanted to go home to his Lord."

I was glad to hear it, but I knew this: my life as I knew it was over. The only thing I had ever wanted since I was 13 had been taken from me. I couldn't imagine going on without him.

When they finally let me inside the room, I walked toward the love of my life on wobbly legs. But before I could reach him, I lost it all over again with heavy sobs and deep, desperate gasps. I sat on Frank's bed and just looked at him. He seemed to wear a slight smile. I slowly ran my finger along the length of his handsome profile, forehead, nose, lips, chin, forehead, nose, lips, chin. Just as he had said that night on his show, his spirit was gone and with the Lord, and his body—not him— was still here. Even so, I couldn't help it. I began kissing him. I kissed his shoulders and his chest, and his arms and hands, feeling his skin under my lips, remembering our oneness, trying to imbed his features in my memory. "You can go now, honey. You can go."

I turned to Marina, who had entered behind me. "A part of me is gone," I said to her.

"But a part of Frank is still here with you," she replied. I suddenly felt a tidal wave of desire to hug my children, the bearers of his DNA. I turned back to Frank and his body confirmed the permanence of his soul's departure. Dark spots started appearing on his skin.

* * *

The morning of the funeral was cold and rainy. The number of people who I anticipated might come, did. Thousands filled the church as well as the campus outside. Dennis Prager, Frank's Salem colleague, was there, so too were Joni Eareckson Tada, Greg Laurie, Dr. Dobson, and Jim Daley. The entire service was going to be simulcast to hundreds of thousands of people around the world. I'm told it could have been in the millions.

My plan was to hold it together for the entire service. My plan failed as soon as Dennis Prager walked up to the dais. Suddenly, as he began to speak, the answer, God's answer to me when I prayed and asked for three things as I laid in the grass 37 years before as a 13-year-old girl, came rushing over me like wind through a window. "Gina, do you see?" God spoke deep into my soul once more. "I gave you everything you asked for." I sat back in shock.

Can Frank fall in love with me? Yes.

Can I marry Frank? Yes.

Can he be loved by thousands? Yes.

Gina Pastore Gallery

Into the Quiet

My mom and I the day of my first communion. We had a party at the house with family and friends.

Dad and I at my high school Father and Daughter Dance.

My Place in the World

Since we eloped, I never had a wedding photo. This picture was taken a couple years after we were married, and is very special to me.

Frank makes it to the big leagues!

Frank was thrilled to be a daddy! Pictured here with our son Frank.

Me and my baby girl! Pictured here with our daughter Christina.

Frank gets his own radio show in Los Angeles, *The Frank Pastore Show*.

Frank loved interviewing Christian leaders, and pastor Greg Laurie became a dear friend.

God's Answer, and Mine

Frank and I on his motorcycle in the parking garage where he worked.

One of our last family photos. We're all together in my son's backyard: Josh, Christina, me, Frank, Frankie, Jessica and Michael. Oh, and Sherlock and Cannoli, our family dogs.

Ghosts and Echoes

It was difficult to take family photos after Frank died. This is at my book celebration party for *Picking Up My Shattered Pieces*. At the time of this photo, I have three grandchildren: Michael, William and Finley.

My mom, me, Christina, Finley and our newest additions, William and Samantha!

Deb Rooney Gallery

As Perfect Storms Go

Mom and dad, 17-year-old lovebirds

Mom, dad, and me

Me, my brother, and sister

Growing up pretty

Confident high schooler

The cutter and future husband

Interruption of a Wedding Plan

Bill and I's wedding photo

Family trips to the great outdoors

Travels with my pilot husband

Erynn, Will, and Patrick

Will and Grandpa airplane

Sean and Jana

Crosses in the Snow

Will was the ring bearer at Sean and Jana's wedding. We had Patrick's vest cut down to fit him, and he wore the belt buckle meant for Patrick too.

Patrick's daughter, Reese Paytin Rooney. She was born March 4, 2009, two months after the accident.

Debbie Siciliani Gallery

My Rapidly Receding Mother

My family

My mom and me

Two Miracle Boys

Our wedding day

Miracle boys

My handsome Nick and me

Jimbo and I

Jimbo's brothers! Steve and Jeff

Our last photo of the Siciliani family of six

Skyfall

The Fab 5 honoring Nick at the celebration of life

Toronto, Out of the Question

My Sister's-in-Christ who were the hands and feet of Jesus!

Meeting Deb Rooney at Camp Widow

Grief, Like a Battle

My beautiful sisters-in-law who comforted me and were always there loving me through my grief.

Jimbo and his beautiful mom. Jimbo adored his mom!

Braided Gallery

New bonus family

Gina, Deb, Debbie and Big Wave Dave's family get to meet.

Debbie meeting her idol,
Big Wave Dave.

Deb and Debbie became special
contributors on Gina's radio show
Real Life.

The "Deb's" and Gina speaking
at their 3rd annual Women's Day
Retreat.

The three of us are bonded and
enjoy a special friendship.

Postscript

Colin and Jessica Rooney next door
to Debbie's friend, Gail, in Idaho.

Love after Loss - Debbie and her
husband, Ron Smallwood.

- Deb Rooney -

Crosses in the Snow

Last: Bill, with son Patrick, is in Colorado to refurbish and ready a barn on their property for son Sean's wedding reception, and has just called home to announce his decision to stay one more night to avoid the high winds in California. The next morning, Deb's sister and brother-in-law have just pulled up on her driveway, on a Sunday morning, unannounced and wearing tragedy on their faces.

Flying with Bill was always a mixed bag. It was full of excitement for the adventure, pride for his accomplishment of getting his license and learning to be such a competent pilot, and fear for all the operational "bugs" of his particular airplane that would occur mid-flight and have him befuddled and trying not to look concerned. That's when he would assure me that flying was the "safest mode of transportation out there," and follow with, "Nothing can really go that wrong, and if anything does, I'm always going to simply return to the airport right away and end the flight. I'm not going to mess around. I promise."

Okay, good.

In the moments when it became clear why my sister, Jackie, and her husband, John, were walking toward me as if each ankle carried a 50-lb. weight, Bill's proclamations of safety and common sense quickly slipped into my thoughts, but they were brief and gone in a flash. Once Jackie tearfully said to me, red-nosed and tissue in hand, "Honey...there's been an accident…they didn't make it," my body began to act without me, falling to the ground, and summoning a noise—half roar, half scream—from somewhere dark in me I never knew existed. I somehow pulled myself off the ground and stumbled to the bathroom, where my body heaved like it might combust and then violently unleashed the contents of my stomach. I fell into a wailing so hard I thought the structure of my body may not have the strength to withstand it. When I exited the bathroom, I frantically paced our home, going round and round, hands wringing, eyes spurting, hoping that in my pacing there might be a figuring-out that what appeared to be the truth wasn't at all, that I might come upon a new truth to supplant the one screaming in my brain. Bill and Patrick couldn't possibly be dead. There was simply no way. I had to figure out how a report of an accident was just a terrible mistake. But each time I passed Jackie and John and saw their tragic faces, they confirmed, as they tried to reach out and comfort me, the truth—my search was in vein. My husband and son were gone and never coming back. And I never even got to say goodbye.

It was snowing in Steamboat Springs, Colorado, that morning. As Bill and Patrick took off around 9 a.m. whatever it was they didn't like about the conditions, be it weather or a malfunctioning of the plane, it seemed Bill did exactly what he told me he would. He appeared to have turned around and headed back to the airport. But at some point the bottom fell out of his plan. Just one mile north of the airport, the plane slammed into the hard, snowy ground and burst into a ball of fire. They both died on impact.

Larry Andrade, the airport manager, came upon the crash site first and knew immediately who it was, having seen Bill and Patrick many times. He called Bill's good pal and realtor, Chuck Armbruster, who called our son Sean, who was in Texas with his fiancée, Jana, at a wedding. Sean had the good sense to call Colin's baseball coach at Pepperdine, who would tell Colin; the parents of Patrick's wife, Erynn, who would tell her; and Jackie and John—so all of us would be told by somebody in person, not over the phone, and at the same time. But as happens, the word got out and within an hour after receiving the news from Jackie, people began showing up at my house—arms outstretched and ready to relay messages of faith, prayer, and a loving God. As I stormed around my house and screamed loud enough to scare the neighbors, hugging friends was the last thing I wanted to do;

their words were the last things I wanted to hear. I wanted to be devastated, ticked off, and sick to my stomach. I wanted to rip my hair from my scalp, knock things off tables, and let my nose run wherever it may. As much as I appreciated each person who came, I did not want to try to control anything about me or my response. If my husband and son just fell out of the sky to their deaths, there was no doubt about it—I was dying, too. It's not something one wants to do with an audience.

The agonizingly slow minutes of the long day ahead found me in my backyard—a place that offered the perfect backdrop to what was going on in my heart. The winds that had raged the day before had turned our yard into a disaster—branches, leaves, overturned umbrellas, and plants were everywhere—and I suffered the long minutes and hours there in my heart's scenic match. Coach Rod, Colin's baseball coach from Pepperdine, sat quietly with me when I entered my home office, put my head on my desk, and cried some more. As more hours passed, he said nothing, knowing there was nothing to say. He was just there. I appreciated him so much.

That evening, Sean and Jana arrived home from Texas and exploded into the house and into my arms, where we held each other and disbelieved together. I held Colin and Sean close, feeling their shoulders in my arms and remembering the miracles of their lives in a way I hadn't for some time.

That night, as we tried to get some sleep, Colin and Sean laid on the ground beside me as I laid on the bed. Jana laid with me, arm around my body and crying deep into the wee hours. She was just Sean's 21-year-old fiancée, yet she suffered our tragedy as if she had been a part of our family forever. I couldn't believe she felt strong enough about me and Bill to have that kind of reaction. In a day that marks my greatest tragedy, Jana's response to the pain stands out as one of the beautiful moments.

When the sun rose, the morning greeted us with a fresh new 24 hours to endure, a minute by minute survival of time and loss—the cruelest assault on a person possible. Embracing Erynn was particularly devastating. Inside her belly that pushed against me as we held each other tight was a little girl who would never know her daddy and grandfather. Just a few months prior, we were on a walk together when she exclaimed, "I love my life!" She had a baby, one on the way, a husband she loved, and our gratitude for making our son such a happy man. Her tears were unbearable for me.

In the days ahead, we made the solemn journey to Steamboat Springs for the purpose of collecting the ashes—collecting their bodies was not an option given the force of the impact and fire. As we approached the airport, I looked out the window toward the crash site and saw two giant crosses had been erected there. Workers from our property, looking for a way to express their condolences, had built and placed the crosses, thereby making the perfect choice. The images were indelible and true. Yes, Bill and Patrick were with God now.

As we traveled like good soldiers to the cemetery, putting one foot in front of the other, wishing we could be doing anything but this, we arrived, entered, and were greeted with two nondescript boxes for transporting. The moment was painfully devoid of any ceremony or fanfare for my spectacular men. Just a few days earlier, Bill had kissed me goodbye and Patrick had given me one of his big love-you-mom embraces. Now they were dull, loveless powder in plastic boxes on a cold table.

On the way back to the airport, the boys wanted to stop off at the crash site to satisfy their need to feel their dad and brother, to stand where they were, to pray and share in the pain the best they could. I stayed in the car—I didn't have it in me to walk the field in search of the wreckage where life turned such a sharp, tragic corner. It was simply more than I could take. The woman of a lonely red farmhouse on the property braved the snowy January conditions and walked to the window of our vehicle to offer her condolences. It was such a fine, caring thing to do. The boys returned with a few remnants from the crash, bits and pieces of the plane. We handed them around and looked and touched them longingly. I believe we were all trying to bring Bill and Patrick close enough to kiss again.

At the airport, we were made to place the boxes of ash, now crammed into backpacks, on the security conveyer belt. With great reluctance approaching moral outrage, I did what I was told. I watched them slowly travel under the X-ray and through to the other side. Bill? Patrick, honey? Can you really be in there?

Nothing seemed real.

When we arrived home, we drove to Erynn's house to deliver Patrick's ashes and, unbeknownst to her, his ring, given to us by the mortuary. When we walked in, friends and family had come to be with her and our entrance into that setting, with a box of ash in hand, had a truly sobering effect on everyone. It could not have been more painful for Erynn to receive her husband home in that condition and to experience the mind warp of trying to conceive that the man she loved was in a container the size of a shoe box. When Erynn's father, Doug, who had traveled with us to Colorado, presented the ring, Erynn and I wept bitterly in each other's arms. Amid all the pain, she was deeply relieved to have his wedding ring again. In a plane filled with things, his wedding ring was the one thing that was not just a thing.

As the shock wore away in the coming days, I began to realize that every aspect of my future was suddenly different, and as it slowly came into view, every projection forward tore away at my mind. I couldn't square any thought of my husband and son being gone with ever being happy again. The two seemed incongruent in every way; no overlap was conceivable.

But then something rather remarkable occurred. Sheila Coleman, a neighbor who happened to be the daughter of the Reverend Robert Shuler, came to the house to perform a process by which true healing could begin. She had developed this process after the shooting at the Crystal Cathedral had compelled her to take action and minister to the victims. With Sean and Colin in the room, Sheila, along with her sisters, who were a part of her ministry, painstakingly took us through a visualization of the event:

the take-off

the realization of a problem

the decision to turn around and head back to the airport

the alarmed conversation that must have occurred when the problem turned potentially greater than they could handle

the panic at the loss of altitude

their final words to each other as the ground rushed forward in their windows.

For the first time, I saw their faces, read their body language, felt their desperation, and heard their words to each other. Suddenly, I was no longer safe at home but in the cockpit, living their nightmare with them, pulling for them, hoping for them, hoping for me. I looked at Sean and Colin in the room with me, their faces wrenched in pain and covered in tears and the contents of each of their noses, and near pleading for it to stop. Our bodies quaking with agony and wanting to get out of that room, there was one more visualization Sheila wanted from us. She wanted us to watch their spirits lift into the air. And so, we did. Before the crash, before their destruction, before they were taken from me, I saw them lift—a beautiful, ghostly ascent, higher and higher into the presence of God. Finally free of this life's struggles and pains, Bill and Patrick settled into the arms of God far away from the bounds of Earth.

It brought a slight smile to my face, and for the first time since the tragedy began, there was a wafting, fragrant peace that fell over my heart. Would it remain for the rest of my life? Or was it fleeting, and therefore had I just embarked on a journey to wrestle it back every day until the end?

- Debbie -

Skyfall

*Last: Jimbo, ailing from the latent effects of so much radiation as a teen
sufferer of cancer, is deteriorating. On a weekend when his brothers have
given him the assignment to pick up some equipment in Laughlin, Nevada,
he views the trip as an opportunity to have a guy's weekend with their two
oldest sons. Debbie doesn't love the idea; his driving has been questionable
lately. But as she consents, she gives Nick, who has just recently shown a new
willingness to share his life with Debbie, the responsibility of keeping his
dad awake during the trip.*

The story of what happened the evening in 2013 when Jimbo,
Nick, and Greg drove from the house on their way to a guys'
weekend in Laughlin, Nevada, has its roots, to some degree, in an event
that occurred all the way back in 1994. That was the year I was given
a book called *Motherless Daughters* by my sister-in-law. Appreciative of
the gift as I was, I knew I just wasn't ready to feel the pain I was sure the
book would ignite. And so, I never read it.

When I was pregnant with Nick two years later, I felt strongly that
Jimbo and I should travel to Lafayette, California, to find and visit the
gravesite of my mother—a place I hadn't been since I was six, when
my dad took me once. As we searched the cemetery grounds, it was
Jimbo who came across my mother's headstone first. He was so cute.
He was out-of-his-mind excited that I would finally get to be alongside

my mother again, the closest I had been to her in 22 years. But when I joined Jimbo at her gravestone and saw her name engraved so boldly, Diana Dean Douglas, I was overcome. Suddenly the idea that she was once actually alive and real hit me. It meant I really did have a mother. I didn't realize how much of my heart was missing until I was standing there with her. I collapsed in Jimbo's arms, sobbing abruptly and uncontrollably—crying straight to 10 with no ramp-up. "Never again," I said. It was way, way too painful.

About a year later, my best friend's mother sent me an article about the Motherless Daughter groups that were springing up all over the country. Still, I couldn't muster the courage to read it. But two years after that, I came across the article after organizing a drawer and suddenly, for some reason, I was ready.

The article made a very good argument for motherless daughters to step into the presence of other motherless daughters to find healing for those parts of themselves they may not even know were left injured. And so, with a girlfriend in tow, I attended a Christmas event where the author of the book was a guest speaker and, I swear it's true, I cried from the moment I walked into that room until the moment I left. These were not co-sufferers in the tragedy of having lost a loved one. These were women who had lost their moms, mostly at a young age—just like me—and had traveled my exact path of pain: dads who married quickly and simply never talked about our mothers again. It was a room full of adult women who were once young girls suffering alone in their beds, crying and wanting to reach out and wrap their arms around their mother's waist, maybe feel their hair being stroked with a soft, loving hand. Our understanding of each other's pain was our sisterhood. I was forever changed. I couldn't wait to go back.

Thirteen years later, I was still attending the group when, one evening, one of the ladies commented on what a different person I was since coming. All the ladies agreed, remarking on how freely my smile spread across my face when I talked about my mom and how I was no longer curled up in a ball of tears. They were right. I was completely different; in many ways, healed. I remember listening to my favorite Christian radio host, Big Wave Dave, on the air talking about a friend of his, also a Christian broadcaster, who suffered a motorcycle accident that had left him in a coma and on the verge of death. I recall thinking that, should the worst happen, his wife would need the comfort of women who had lost their husbands in as close to the same way as possible to be able to heal. I knew the power of a shared experience. And I believe my entire time spent with Motherless Daughters was God healing and thereby preparing me for what was to come six months later, when Jimbo and the boys climbed aboard our truck and started on their way to Laughlin.

Two hours had passed since they had left. I picked up the phone to call Jimbo, who I estimated to be about half way to Laughlin by then. He answered and gave me a quick update on their progress. As suspected, he was somewhere in the middle of the California desert, maybe around Newberry Springs off highway 40, making good time with the boys doing fine. We talked for a minute or two. "Okay," I said, "just checking in, honey. Thanks! Call me when you get there."

"Will do. I love you."

"I love you, too."

Of course, I wasn't just checking in, not at all. A phone call from me to my husband on a long trip with my boys in the car was me securing and re-securing the locking mechanism to my heart so that I would never again have to feel what I felt as a little girl when Mom died and essentially disappeared.

When 10:23 p.m. rolled around and no one had called to tell me they had arrived—something they were very aware I wanted—I texted each and received no reply. And so I called each of them, but nobody answered. I suddenly felt a shot of heat go through my body like a blast from a flame thrower. I called Harrah's hotel, where they were going to be staying.

"No, Mr. Siciliani has not checked in as of yet," the girl at the front desk said.

"Hmm. I hope they didn't get into an accident," I offered. I hung up and broke into a sweat. "No, no, no. Don't go there," I implored myself. "Just wait for the phone call. It'll come. There's a reason."

At 10:45, after 10 fearful minutes, the phone rang.

"Finally!" I said. I looked at the screen. It read "Hospital."

Hospital?

"Hello?"

"Are you Greg Siciliani's mother?" the man on the other end of the line said.

"Yes."

"Ma'am, I'm calling . . . I wanted to let you know Greg is okay and he's with me. But unfortunately there has been an accident."

My heart began to thump hard against my chest.

"Your husband was going at high speeds when his truck hit gravel and swerved and then as he tried to gain control, the truck rolled, we think four times. They airlifted Greg. He's okay, but—"

"No! No! No!" I yelled out and crumbled to the ground.

What happened next is not exactly clear. The words that came from his mouth blurred into a jumble of sounds from which I could only pull a few for my mind to process: Nick—dead. Greg found outside the truck. Jimbo found alive against the truck—but died. It felt like he was talking in slow motion and in hyper-speed all at once. Everything in me begin to lock up. "It can't be. This can't be," I said. But it could. It all made sense. They hadn't arrived 45 minutes after they should have. All of them weren't answering texts. All of them weren't answering phone calls. Jimbo was prone to driving mistakes. Now a man from the hospital was calling with catastrophic news.

God, no!

He began to tell me the name of the trauma center—a peculiar name, and in the scramble to navigate the finding of a pen and paper, listen while he spoke, and try to comprehend what he was saying with my body falling deeper into shock, nothing penetrated.

"I CAN'T UNDERSTAND YOU!"

"I CAN'T UNDERSTAND YOU!"

I heard myself scream into the phone hard enough to feel my throat tear. "WHAT WAS THE NAME OF THE HOSPITAL?!"

"SAY IT AGAIN!"

"PLEASE SAY IT AGAIN!" And yet I couldn't receive it. If he hung up I would have no way to find Greg.

"GIVE ME YOUR CELL NUMBER!"

"GIVE ME YOUR CELL NUMBER!"

I hung up and came unglued, screaming with my face against the carpet.

I quickly called my mother-in-law. "JIMBO AND NICK ARE DEAD!" I howled into the phone. Chelsie, 11, heard the screaming and ran to where I was.

"What's going on?"

I looked at her face with my own ready to implode. "YOUR DADDY

AND NICK HAVE DIED!"

The flood of terror that rushed around my body rose quickly to well above my head when I looked into the eyes of my daughter who was collapsing in horror. I grabbed her and we ran downstairs to Sammy and I told him what had happened. I held him in my arms while seated on the stairs. His little eyes crossed with confusion. At six, he was the exact same age as me when I lost my mom—my nightmare come true. The last thing I wanted for my kids was for them to taste any of the pain that I had.

Chelsie bellowed, "Now who's going to walk me down the aisle?" and burst into more wailing. I grabbed both of them and looked intensely in their eyes.

"No, no, no. Listen to me! God's got us! He hasn't left us! He's going to take care of us! You have to trust Him! Trust, trust, trust!"

In just a few minutes, the doorbell rang and it was my sister-in-law, Jeannette. "I told you! I told you!" I yelled at her when I saw her standing there. Two weeks prior we were together and had posed this question to each other: "What would we do if our husbands died?" to which I felt compelled to say, "It'll probably happen to me first."

Jeannette stepped inside, took me in her arms, and held me while I quaked. I didn't know it, but she was a harbinger of things to come. Over the next 10 excruciating hours, through calls and social media, person after person, friends—including my three dearest friends, Gail, Aimee, and Diane—family, and plenty of folks I didn't know, came to my door and into my life to pray with me and hold me close as I wept bitterly in their arms. It was a steady stream of provision that I cannot explain. Perfectly timed to pick up where the previous visitor left off, each had the same thing in mind: to offer me their embrace, prayers, and tears. It did not escape me that a miracle was taking place: all the people who learned about our tragedy were compelled to action, to be Jesus to me. It wasn't just a bunch of folks who got the news and chose to sit at home wringing their hands and thinking, *Oh dear.* They got up, came over, and entered into my pain. Like angels, they ascended on my home through the night and into the morning. When one was holding me, the others filled my rooms, where they prayed and tended to my kids. I was able to hold two of God's provisions in my mind: that He was delivering just what I needed, and that He had prepared me for this time. I can't imagine heaping the loss of my husband and son on top of my open motherless wounds. I would have drowned. It was so prevalent in my mind that when my dad walked into the house to console me in the early, sleepless hours of the next morning, I told him sternly, "I will never do what you did to me, Dad! I'm going to talk about Jimbo and Nick to the kids. We're going to celebrate their lives."

When my two brothers-in-law, Jeff and Steve, found out, they happened to be in Northern California at the time and jumped on a plane to make their way to Las Vegas where Greg had been airlifted and where I was headed. When they arrived, they needed my consent to make some decisions about Greg on my behalf. The head nurse called me to get it, and as she did she attempted to tell me about Greg's condition. "NO! DO NOT TELL ME ANYTHING ABOUT GREG!" I screamed. I wasn't making a decision. My body was merely reacting, and it could not take any more tragic news. My beloved husband and son were lying dormant and cool in a morgue somewhere in San Bernardino. I could not listen to any kind of description about loss of limbs or eyes or anything to my poor Greg. I knew he was alive and I was going to let that be my one saving grace. Information about his wrecked and ruined body as he was lying in the ICU, where they said he was, was not an option. I needed him to be perfect in my mind to get me through the next hours of flying into my own personal hell.

"You don't want to know how your son is doing?" the nurse asked incredulously.

"NO, I DO NOT!" I shrieked as I threw my phone to the ground.

The plane ride to Las Vegas was torture. The head flight attendant rather fancied himself a standup comedian and regaled the passengers with every joke he knew. He kept everyone laughing—but not me. The constant laughter as a backdrop to my catastrophe was more than I could take. It drove me to my knees, each laugh like a flame licking at my mind.

When I arrived at the hospital, my brother-in-law met me in front and promptly told me that Greg was essentially as good as ever, just a few scratches. "Then why did they have him in the ICU?"

"They were just being extra cautious, I guess," he said.

Over the objections of some family members, I had taken the kids with me to Vegas and as we turned the corner to see Greg in his room, the first words out of his mouth were, "Is Sammy here?" Sammy ran to Greg and jumped up onto his bed and into his arms where they cried together. I would later learn that when Steve delivered the news to Greg about his brother and dad, Jeff had to turn his back—he couldn't watch Greg, just 13, fall that far into mournful lament. How Greg needed Sammy at that moment. I was so glad to not have disappointed him.

Of course, nothing could dampen the pain of what was happening to all of us: being in a hospital to gather my son and bring him home with half his family missing. I wondered how he would survive it.

The trauma center administrator came to me with a piece of paper that I would have to sign to release Jimbo's and Nick's bodies from the San Bernardino morgues to the one in Corona del Mar, near our home. I knew that their names would be displayed on the documentation and went weak-kneed at the thought of having to see them filling the blanks of some cold transfer template. Jeff had to do his best to fold the paper just so, so that all I could see was the blank space for me to sign my name. I scribbled a few loops, threw down the pen, and lost it.

Finally it came time to identify Jimbo and Nick, but it didn't take long to decide that wasn't going to happen. My brothers-in-law could make the identifications, or somebody, but not me. As a woman of only 44, I had too many years left to battle the images that would be imprinted on my mind in that morgue—my beautiful son and husband in some manner of terrible disrepair. I had to keep my memory of them untouched. I simply didn't want any competing images.

And so, I didn't go. And I didn't and don't regret it. I said my good-byes to them where I stood crying, with their perfect faces in my mind, just a few miles from where they were lying peacefully now in the morgue, eyes closed, and gone.

* * *

Two caskets were just beyond the stage steps as I stood at the podium of our church before 1,500 friends and family and did the unthinkable, at least for me; I eulogized my own son and husband. It was something that had sprung to mind in the days preceding even though it was very unlike me to do something like that. But my desire to stand before all those faces and speak was so strong I knew it had to be God prompting me. At least for Jimbo, I'm the only one who could honor him the way he deserved.

Without notes, just following however God might lead, I talked for 20 minutes, and there were lots of smiles and plenty of laughs, which were strangely fitting for two lovable characters like Jimbo and Nick, even as we said goodbye. I concluded the talk with a thumbs-up, Nick's constant and ever-present expression to all, and the entire church returned their thumbs-up in reply. As I walked off, I was given a standing ovation. They were not clapping for a good performance. They were heaping on agreement that these were two lives worthy of so many smiles, laughs, and tears—a celebration, as the program in each of their hands said. Battle Scars Bromance, the lip-synch video made by Nick and the Fab Five, the one he was so eager to show me, played on the large screen. Each remaining member, now the Fab Four, sat with me tightly on the floor and tried to let the glory of friendship, at least for a few minutes, be a healing balm on the pain of Nick being taken from them, from us all. When our pastor read from a Facebook post that Nick had written one year earlier, "Be thankful for each day because you never know if tomorrow will be your last," my little niece, Amanda, ran to me and curled up in my lap as if she couldn't stand seeing me cry one more tear without doing something about it.

Earlier, Chelsie had sung "Sky Fall" a "song for Daddy" from his favorite Bond movie. I was feeling good and strong with so many people around me who loved my family, but I knew in the days to come, when life without Jimbo and Nick would set in, the sky would fall for me.

That is how I knew I had one task that I could not shrink from for the good of my kids and sanity: to find and step into the embrace of one woman who had lost her husband and son, taken from her at the very same time. It was the only way I would survive.

Part 4
The Aftermath

- Gina -

Ghosts and Echoes

Last: Frank dies four weeks to the day after his motorcycle accident, the exact incident he unwittingly used as a metaphor to drive home a spiritual point on his radio show the day of the crash. At the funeral, looking at all the people in attendance, plus knowing that the entire service was broadcast to hundreds of thousands of people around the world, Gina realizes that God had answered her prayer, the one she made in the grass of her backyard in 1974 when she was 13 years old.

It made perfect sense that in the days following Frank's funeral, my kids and close friends would want to spend the night with me. I would do the same thing if I was in their shoes. And I appreciated it; I most certainly did. I loved them for it. But as I laid there in the dark, knowing that somebody who cared for me deeply was in the next room, the temporary nature of their stay was all I could think about. "One day soon, things will have to get back to normal," I would say to myself. "One day soon." What was meant to be a comfort was, but at the same time, it brought about its own pain. It was a reminder of the torture that was coming the day they would leave and I would shut the door behind them and be alone with the thick, slow quiet and emptiness of our home, and ghosts of Frank around every corner.

They didn't take long to appear.

Once I was alone, I would "see" Frank in the shower, or sitting at his desk, or in his favorite chair in front of the TV. I would walk around the corner and there he would be, fridge open, digging into the drawers looking for something to eat. Or I would look out the back window and see him, bandana on his head, pulling weeds like he loved to do. It was like I was trying to heal from Frank's death while living in the Frank Museum. But the torment didn't stop there.

His beloved books were on the shelves; the spines' colors seemed louder than before. His favorite coffee mug sat in its spot toward the end of our kitchen counter, and I was ever mindful of its presence, cooking and cleaning around it (I didn't move it for five years). His favorite chair rested with great presence in front of the TV and seemed to call out to him to come and sit down and cozy up with a blanket. Day after day the echoes of Frank only seemed to grow louder. I would constantly anticipate—almost like I could hear it—the sound of the front door opening and closing, and Frank's voice calling out, "Honey, I'm home!" I was painfully aware I was eating alone and preparing food for me, just me. I would look across our kitchen table at an empty chair as my head oscillated in disbelief. I would go to bed and lay his giant pillow beside me and put the covers over it so it felt like his body was there. Pictures of Frank, Frank's clothes, his tools, his aftershave—he was in every part of the house like my mind was stuck on a loop, willing him to be there as I embraced his memory and pushed it away in the same motion.

One afternoon the torment got so bad I began to wilt. Frank was nowhere but everywhere. I ran into the garage, hit the opener, and ran down the driveway toward my neighbors, Mark and Judy. "Hi, Gina," Mark said surprised as he saw me running, something I never did.

"Mark, hi, I can't be in there anymore," I said, tears streaming down my face. "Frank is all over my house. I can't go back in."

Mark seemed to understand immediately. He invited me into their living room, where I sat and rocked and, face in hands, wept that the home I loved had become uninhabitable. He brought me bottled water and waited patiently, doing the right thing: not offering words of comfort or advice. He simply sat there while I summoned the courage to get up and go back to carry on the fight against my memories and imagination. I wondered if it was going to happen again. How many times would I find myself running in a full sprint from my own house?

No place seemed safe from his memory. I drove to Stater Bros., our grocery store, and walked the aisles until I realized I was in the cottage cheese aisle. Cottage cheese was Frank's go-to; he ate it nearly every day at lunch with a sandwich I would make him. He loved it. I grabbed my purse and ran out of the store, leaving the cart where it was. I sat in my car crying and shaking my head at the finality of my predicament. *A lifetime of this? God, what have you done?*

I sat with the wife of my pastor in a back room of the church and watched the services on a monitor for a full six weeks before I was ready to go out into the sanctuary and receive the sympathetic looks that I knew were coming, and dreaded. I found a rather inconspicuous spot in our large church and sat in the very last row, far away from the seats that made up Frank's and my regular spot. I denied all invitations to join friends and kept my head slightly angled so I couldn't tell if people were occupying "our" seats, center right, along the aisle. One wrong turn of my head and I might just see folks there, or worse yet, ghosts of me and Frank sitting closely together doing what we did every Sunday, enjoying God and each other. Landmines were everywhere.

I noticed that I still felt very married. It never even occurred to me to take off my ring (I still haven't). But I wasn't married—or was I? If I wanted to be married to Frank for the rest of my life, couldn't I just claim my commitment to him would continue till the day we were reunited? Did I have to be a widow?

One day, as I remembered what Dennis Prager had said when he spoke at Frank's funeral, I figured out why I was going to bed earlier and earlier, often by 8 p.m. As Dennis stood at the lectern of our church, he mentioned that he wasn't supposed to work on a high holy day, which it was at the time, but then he talked about grief being "work," so it would be hard for him, at that moment, not to work.

Yes, it is. Grief is work. It is extraordinarily exhausting work. From the moment I woke up to the moment I laid my head down and drifted to sleep, I was busy warding off the feeling of missing Frank and that my life had come to an end. I was averaging about three breakdowns an hour, each a crushing blow. That is how sleep became my respite, my sanctuary, one I sought earlier and earlier in the day. Besides, Frank had a way of making appearances in my sleep; reoccurring dreams where he would walk in the door and I would call out, "Frank! Where have you been? We have to get you to the station! They're waiting for you!" And then he would take me and hold me and I could feel him again. In his leather riding jacket, his strong arms would wrap tightly around me.

Life did not offer me Frank in the flesh. Only sleep did. Waking up was near hell but worth every moment. Because on a good night, my Frank walked through the doors and into my arms—the only thing I ever wanted.

- Deb Rooney -

The Moon's Still There

Last: After Bill and Patrick arrive home in boxes of ash, Deb and her two sons are led through a projection and imagining process of the steps of the crash, as well as "seeing" them lift into heaven.

It's awful how many times I would find myself sitting alone with my head subtly moving left to right as I stared—the endless back and forth of disbelief, but also confusion as to how I was going to grieve both Bill and Patrick at the same time. One death left my heart crushed, which meant there was nothing left for the other—and yet there had to be. I loved them both more than I loved myself.

And so I remained in a state of in-between, unable to give either face the focus it required. The heart simply can't grieve in two directions at the same time—it's just not made that way. It brought me to my knees over and over again as I searched for a way to miss them both, but who to miss when?

I still can't quite make sense of it.

Stores became my necessary evil. I would venture out to the supermarket or Home Depot, and people walking to and fro in the middle of their own thoughts and tasks had a strange power over me. I was at once happy to hear hustle and bustle break up the monotony of my painfully quiet life, but it also made me want to stomp my foot and scream, "Don't you care that my husband and son just died?" How dare they be so rude to simply walk past.

What they didn't seem to understand was that I would be going home to a house filled floor to ceiling with a heavy, oppressive sense of absence. In every direction there was more of it, every room, every chair, every tick of the clock. Bill not here. Bill not coming. Bill gone forever. And it was taking a terrible toll. The simplest chores that I never had to perform before were suddenly backbreaking—not because I couldn't do them, but because they required that I walk in Bill's shoes, following his steps to a T. I didn't want to go there. I didn't want to walk the path between rooms to collect the trash bins, take them out to our trash cans, empty them, and then roll the cans out to the street. I was walking in Bill's air, experiencing him with every step. It was just emptying out the trash, a ten-minute chore, but it became my Mt. Everest.

I kept on subconsciously feeling like there would be some place to hide, that I would come across it somehow, that somewhere there was a respite from the tsunami of pain rushing all around me. Higher ground of some sort. A sturdy pole to cling to. A boat to ride it out. But there simply was none. There is no way to outrun it. Little by little it began to dawn on me that pain was my new reality. Pain and I were starting to feel one and the same.

There was sleep, of course. Sleep brought moments of rest and pause, and that was good. But sleep also brought about those waking moments, when reality slowly reappears, like a mist passing from view to leave the harsh lines and edges of life to stare at—and remember. Real life would come back, and dreams of Bill, and especially of Patrick, whose light-hearted appearances through the night were so joyous, would vanish for another 18 hours.

I learned that 18 hours is a long, long time.

With Patrick and Erynn's house just a few blocks down the street, I would drive the two minutes to their place, not walk—I couldn't. Walking would give me too much time on the same path Patrick would take with Will in the baby backpack, when he would bring him to our house to play. Once there, I could spend each evening with Erynn, have dinner, give Will a bath, and then sit with Erynn and grieve together. They were such hard, beautiful times; the sweet memories that made us laugh and the quaking shoulders of missing.

Upon leaving Erynn's the first night we were together, the moon sat with bold presence in the night, as if it were telling me it was positioned outside her front door for a good reason. I watched it carefully as I drove home.

The next night as I left Erynn's, I took notice of it again. And then I began looking for it each night as I walked out of the house, keeping it in my window as I drove. I kept my eye on the moon every night, as it changed places and shapes. That is when it began to speak to me. The consistency of it started to fill my heart with a confidence that as long as it was going to be in the sky, God was going to be there too, orchestrating its perfect placement. "The moon's still there," I would say to myself each night. I looked forward to it.

Of course, as soon as I entered my empty house upon returning, the tears would flow again until my face turned red and puffy and my eyes were irreparably blurry. I would sit in my office and cry until I got up, got ready for bed, and laid myself down in a bed I felt too small to occupy. *Come, Bill and Patrick, visit me again. I beg you, please.*

During the days, I journaled feverishly, making entries that were not so much about where I found myself, but long paragraphs that were essentially letters to Bill, telling him how much I missed him, and even asking him things—from deep questions about his love for me, to what really took place in the cockpit that awful morning, to how to turn on the sprinklers.

A year later, I returned to Bible study and took particular notice, as we studied James, of how consistently the Word makes mention that for those who are in Christ, no protection from trial is promised. In fact, trials can be expected, and it is during those times that God draws particularly close.

It's the kind of thing that brings about a sharp, dual response. I longed for God to draw close, but at the same time I pushed Him away. I'd rather have Bill home with me and Patrick home with his family.

But it was there, in the middle of my catastrophe, that James began to open me to the idea that I was suffering alongside my Lord, who also knew the pain of terrible loss of relationship. Jesus grieved. In the same way that Erynn greeted me with arms outstretched and tears in her eyes born of pain and loss, my Lord stood with arms outstretched, tears in His eyes too—"Man of Sorrows," as He is described in Isaiah 53. I began to feel moments of profound intimacy with God. Pain was actually refining me and bringing me into greater relationship with Him. Whereas I believed the pain I felt from the loss of Bill and Patrick had reached the deepest part of me, I began to feel God's love reach even deeper. He had found my heart's core in a way nothing else could. I came to an impossible place of joyous grieving.

I soon began to notice my journal entries written to Bill were starting to become less and less frequent, until they ultimately went away altogether. I had begun using the journal to pray to God, who was drawing closer and closer still. Bill was becoming more distant, it is true. But where one might think I was forgetting Bill, I wasn't at all. God, healing me more every day, was simply moving to the fore of my thinking. And it felt so good.

I began to think the sense of purpose that had been brewing in my heart since returning to Bible study might best be manifested by starting a grief ministry at a local church. On a few occasions I had been asked by friends to meet with other grievers, such as the time I was asked to meet with a woman whose husband, a Christian broadcaster, had recently died after a motorcycle accident. Of course I agreed to it. I really wanted to be used. I always had a sense that grievers needed to find like-grievers, those who have experienced the same kind of loss. It was something I longed for too—couldn't get my mind off it, actually—even though finding a woman who lost a husband and son at the same time seemed nearly impossible.

And so I decided to see how God might bless my efforts to start a grief ministry, especially now that I was feeling stronger in Him. Even so, on the first night, at the very first meeting, I opened our time together by playing a touching video—and I lost it. There I was, the one who was supposed to lead these men and women into healing, on the floor, unable to get up. Perhaps it was a good first lesson, at least I hope it was. You never get over it. It never goes away.

- Debbie -

Grief, Like a Battle

Last: Debbie realizes the years spent as a member of the Motherless Daughters was God preparing her for the accident that took Jimbo and Nick. As a result of the group's influence, she feels even more certain that the only way she will survive is if she can find a woman who has lost a husband and son at the same time.

I'm not sure how i knew it. In fact, I'm not sure I knew anything for certain in the dark days following Jimbo and Nick's celebration-of-life service when I walked into my new normal with part of my heart missing. But instinctively, something in my soul told me in my case, grief was not going to be a matter of waiting, or enduring, the painful hours. It was going to be war, a minute by minute battle against the enemy who was going to try to take advantage of my weakened state. And I couldn't let that happen. If I didn't fortify myself against a rock and raise a sword of defiance, I'd get swept away, never to return. I was devastated and on the ground at the loss of my Jimbo and Nick—which meant I was easy pickin' for the devil.

It didn't help that I learned when the paramedics arrived at the crash site, they saw Jimbo alive and leaning against the truck but ran to Greg, who they speculated must have been thrown from the vehicle. Their assumption was he was the one who needed the most help. As it turned out, only Jimbo was dying. Had they given Jimbo attention, they might have been able to save him. The possibility that he was just a different decision away from surviving the crash plagued my mind and pulled me toward despair. Adding to the mental torment was the thought that Jimbo might've been able to live, but watching Nick die was too much for his heart. And so, when Nick died, I think it's possible that Jimbo, so in love with his son, simply let go.

So I gathered my best friends and told them, like I was pleading for my life, that if I was going to make it, I would need them to stay with me, to be by my side every minute, that I simply might drown in pain without eyes to look into or arms to hold me or voices to speak hope and truth. I would never survive the force of the silence without Jimbo's or Nick's voices in our home. Like good sisters in Christ, they did exactly as I asked. Every day and night, a different friend stayed with me so that when I woke up, a living, breathing, praying body was there. I know it was demanding, but the truth was this: be with me or lose me. It was as simple as that.

Of course, I had to do my part. I might awaken in a state of sobbing, but I was determined to get up from my bed each morning, take a shower, put on clothes, and walk out of my bedroom, down the stairs, and into the house. I refused to lie in bed and stay in my pajamas—clothes of the dying. I had three surviving kids. I had to stay alive.

And so that's what I did. Every morning, on unsteady legs and with a face full of tears, I presented myself as a non-target for the enemy. I might have been on the floor crying at some point of every hour, but a pair of jeans, a shirt, and a brush through my hair were my counter-offensive. "You're not going to destroy me," I told the enemy.

One afternoon, I saw Sammy's teacher and told her of my daily routine. "You mean, you haven't stayed in bed one day yet?" she said.

"No."

"Debbie, I laid in bed crying for days!"

"Over my tragedy? Well, you did it for me then—thank you."

Dressing myself every day was one move I did successfully, but truthfully, as I stood before the rest of my day, or my life, I had no idea how I was going to get through. I was nonfunctional in nearly every way. I had to rely on my friends to make dinners; I couldn't string enough consistent thoughts together to complete a recipe before breaking down and falling to the floor. I couldn't walk into my own bathroom without losing it—too many memories of my silly husband crammed into a bathtub and smiling at me as he liked to do. Without Jimbo, I couldn't go to church alone. I couldn't walk near Nick's bedroom without falling apart. I couldn't drive the kids around to friends or different events—I didn't trust myself on the road. I couldn't have the TV on in the house—Jimbo loved watching TV and the sound of it sent me reeling.

That is why after getting up and getting dressed, I concluded I had really only one task for each day: to inject Jesus into my veins. His Word is life, and light, and hope, and I knew if I had any chance of surviving, it would be because I allowed Him to breathe life into me, to remake me at the cellular level. There was no other way; no outside force or philosophy was strong enough. I clung to Jesus with a white-knuckled grip, like holding onto the edge of a cliff. It was Him or nothing. "SAVE ME, LORD! SAVE ME!" I would scream over and over again.

I read the Bible, letting it wash over me day and night, as well as devotionals such as *Jesus Calling*—whose Jesus-is-talking-to-you format meant everything to me. I put Christian music on in the house and sat and cried at the truths in the lyrics, especially each reminder that Jesus had a plan for my life and would reward my faith by drawing near. Jeremy Camp's *Walk by Faith* had me in a ball of tears on the couch:

> I will walk by faith even when I cannot see
> because this broken road Prepares Your will for me
> Help me to rid my endless fears
> You've been so faithful for all my years
> With one breath You make me new
> Your grace covers all I do

A friend encouraged me to keep a journal and write down every time God stepped in and made Himself known. It was a brilliant idea. If I was going to pray for God's presence, then I was going to take those moments and build them like a monument to the faithfulness of God. I needed to remind myself at all times that little by little, act by act, God, and everything about Him, was becoming my new reality. My old life, and whoever I was, was over.

One day, one of my friends who had stayed with me for the night had had to leave early in the morning. When I stepped outside my bedroom to make my way downstairs, her absence, and the quiet of the house, was almost more than I could bear. As I gingerly descended, holding the banister tightly, I turned on the landing midway down the staircase to find another friend, one of the Fab Five mothers, standing on the bottom floor looking at me—someone I was not expecting. Our eyes met and I abruptly stopped. She mistook it as disapproval.

"Debbie!" she said. "Was I not supposed to let myself in?"

After sobbing in her embrace and thanking her for coming, I grabbed my journal and began writing feverishly. My journal was becoming my life's blood.

One day a girlfriend forwarded me "A Letter from Heaven" by Alena Hakala Meadows:

> When tomorrow starts without me
> And I'm not there to see;
> If the sun should rise and find your eyes
> All filled with tears for me
>
> I wish so much you wouldn't cry
> The way you did today;
> While thinking of the many things
> we didn't get to say
>
> I know how much you love me
> As much as I love you;
> And each time you think of me,
> I know you'll miss me too
>
> When tomorrow starts without me
> Don't think we're far apart
> For every time you think of me
> I'm right here in your heart

After pulling myself up off the ground and raising my hands to God in gratitude, I grabbed my journal again.

When I realized that I was sleeping through the night, that the prayers of my friends and family were protecting me from the forces that might attack me as I tried to sleep, I reached for my journal once more. I continued to build my monument of gratitude, and every time

I did, I felt like I could live another hour.

"God is going to bring me somebody who has lost a husband and a son. I just know it!" I began to tell my friends, but was also telling myself. It was part of the battle, to keep myself going, to believe that God was going to come through with what He had set in motion through Motherless Daughters: the comfort and healing that come from a shared exact experience. I needed someone who knew perfectly the depths of my specific catastrophe. "He has to do it," I told myself and anyone who would listen. "He's already spoken to my heart that it's the key to my healing."

Yet, for every good and confident feeling, many new battles came into view. There was the problem of my children and how I, shattered like a glass pitcher, was going to lead them through such extraordinary heartache and longing for their brother and dad. I did some things well and some things I did very poorly. Like the time, as I tried to remedy my father's awful decision of never mentioning my mother to me again, I talked about Nick one too many times to the kids. Greg's face turned tomato-red and he suddenly burst into tears and shaking rage. "Mom, you don't understand! I watched Nick die! I watched him take his last breath!" He was claiming ownership of that territory. All talk about the event was suddenly off limits. I felt terrible that I had dragged him through his personal hell over and over again.

Then there was the matter of June.

June became an awful month in my life when my mother died in June, and I carried with me the pain of that month since childhood. But when my blind date with Jimbo occurred in June and so did our engagement, as well as our wedding, it rescued June for me—no longer was there a black hole in the calendar to have to emotionally prepare for each year. However, with Jimbo's and Nick's passing on June 28, June was once again, now even more than before, ruined. As it approached on the calendar in 2014, I could feel it looming.

But this time I had a plan.

The FISH Fest, my favorite Christian radio station's annual summer concert, was soon coming—in June. I had never gone before and I figured it was time to reclaim June and build new positive emotions around it. I grabbed Chelsie and told her, "We're going to FISH Fest and we're going to keep going. It's going to cost us $500 but I don't care!"

When we arrived at the concert and took our seats, we were in the middle, right down in front. Any closer and we'd be in the show. When the concert was to begin, out walked Master of Ceremonies Big Wave Dave, the FISH personality who I had come to love for his humor and wisdom, as well as his month-long heartfelt plea, a few years prior, to pray for his friend, a fellow Christian broadcaster who ultimately died from injuries sustained in a motorcycle accident on his way home from his show. It was a tragic saga I felt a part of as a prayerful listener, and one I would never forget. I had never even made the connection that Big Wave Dave might make an appearance at the concert, but once I laid eyes on him, it was a joyful moment for me, a much-needed light to brighten my day.

I didn't have my gratitude journal with me to write it down. But without knowing it, a bit of my future had just come into view, something that was worthy of a monument to God if there ever was one. Words such as "gratitude" can hardly express it.

Part 5
The Braiding

- *Gina* -
My Introduction to Make

"Hello?"

"Gina, hi, I have a question for you," said my friend since high school in a midmorning call.

"What?"

"I've asked this woman I know, Deb Rooney, if she would meet with you. She lost her husband and son in a plane crash a few years ago. She knew about Frank's accident too. I thought it might be good for you to get to know her, you know, to be with someone who knows what you're going through."

"Who is she again? How do you know her? Never mind. Yes. I'll meet her."

It had been five months since Frank passed away and I had found my return to feeling good again, or healing, or anything like it, to be going molasses slow—no real progress to speak of at all. That's why the idea of meeting my friend's friend, a fellow "baseball mother," as she explained it, sounded so good to me. She would be someone who might understand my specific sadness—but more than understand, she would recognize and know intimately the reason for every tear. The thought of looking into the eyes of Deb Rooney, whoever she was, deepened my breathing just a bit. Not having to explain myself and yet still be fully known sounded like a bit of heaven. Better yet, the more I thought about it, the more I recalled that I had actually heard about the Rooney tragedy. In fact, Frank and I had even prayed for them.

The afternoon came when I was to meet with Deb Rooney and I was so excited. In a booth in a Cheesecake Factory in Brea, California, was someone who could, just by sitting across the table not saying a word, save me from another night of feeling so incredibly alone and isolated. As the hostess walked me around to where Deb Rooney and my friend were, I turned the corner to see her sitting casually and in mid-laugh as she moved her brown hair from her face. It stopped me. *You mean, I'm going to laugh again?* I thought. My eyes pooled with tears that began their descent by the time I arrived at the table. But it was just the beginning. When Deb saw me, she stood and offered her arms and I sank into them immediately. We both cried together, heads on shoulders, having hardly even said hello.

The rest of the evening was light breaking into my world, like a dungeon floor receiving its first ray of sun. I felt warm and inspired and encouraged about the future—that I would even have one. I told Deb about how Frank's station, KKLA, had talked to me about doing my own radio show, and she told me about taking over Bill's spot at the helm of their large company. We spoke about our need for Jesus, and she confirmed the road ahead would be both seemingly impossible to travel, and illuminated by rays of grace by a God who draws closer than one can imagine.

Suddenly, everything felt doable. Just her smile alone closed a million loops in my mind.

* * *

Veronica Roggemann has been a close friend ever since we met at a Bible study many years ago. Her lovely daughter, Amie, was a teacher at a local elementary school, and one day Veronica invited me to come along with her to visit Amie. She wanted me to see her extraordinary talents for decorating her classroom, and then we'd head to dinner at the beach. It sounded like a terrific way to spend an afternoon to me.

So there we were in the school office before venturing to Amie's class when all of a sudden Veronica nudged me. I looked at her. She was wordlessly and inconspicuously pointing to the woman standing directly in front of me who was talking to a school administrator. Veronica's eyes were saying, "That's her."

I suddenly figured out what she was trying to say. The woman standing two feet from me, a vivacious blonde, was the one Veronica had recently told me about, Debbie Siciliani, a mother at the school whom Amie knew had lost a husband and a son when their truck spun out of control on a highway in the desert. Veronica not only thought I could offer Debbie support and encouragement, but she also knew about my life-changing meeting and subsequent friendship with Deb Rooney and was putting two and two together. Of course! She was right! Debbie Siciliani needed to meet me so I could introduce her to Deb Rooney and they could support each other in their husband-and-son loss. It was up to me to make the introduction.

I looked at Debbie Siciliani, just an arm's length away. I could have just tapped her on the shoulder. But as I debated how to go about getting her attention, she seemed to be rather occupied with the school administrator for the moment, and also, was what I was about to say appropriate for the middle of a crowded school office?

In my hesitation, the moment seemed to pass, and suddenly Debbie was out of the office and we were on our way to Amie's classroom. Did I blow it?

That afternoon, Veronica encouraged Amie to reach out to Debbie, which she did. "Debbie, if you're still on campus, there's someone I'd like you to meet," Amie texted Debbie.

"Sorry, just left" was her reply.

And that is where the matter was left. Veronica continued to encourage Amie to reach out to Debbie, but as busy days go, no contact was ever made. If Debbie Siciliani was ultimately going to meet Deb Rooney, it would have to be something apart from me. God would have to do it.

At least that was my prayer.

- Deb Rooney -

An Easy Volunteer

One of the extraordinary things about deep, catastrophic loss is how differently the Word of God sits up from the page in light of your despair. Each word, because you are so desperate to feel differently than you currently do, has the potential, it must, to bring some solace to your achy soul. And so you read, perhaps like you should have all along, like each word is a life raft.

That is why when I came across 2 Corinthians 1:3-4 the words jumped out at me like a pop-up book, beckoning my attention as never before "Blessed be the God and Father of our Lord Jesus Christ, the Father of mercies and God of all comfort, who comforts us in all our affliction so that we will be able to comfort those who are in any affliction with the comfort with which we ourselves are comforted by God" (NASB).

There it is, I thought. *Purpose.*

The idea that God is calling those who are in Him to comfort the way we have been comforted was a terrific thing to roll over and over in my mind. The call aligned perfectly with who I was. A volunteer at heart, I was easy with adding my name to a list—and I knew the perfect one.

In 2009, Erynn and I had attended a Camp Widow weekend event, the first for each of us, hungry to absorb anything that might make us feel better—anything. Camp Widow is a secular organization, a Soaring Spirits International program, but that was good with us. If they could help, we were there.

The weekend with Camp Widow was a beautiful experience, giving all of us attendees the next best thing to actually having our spouses back from the grave: the closeness in each other's arms, understanding, and words of positivity and love. God's work, it seemed.

In time I began attending Camp Widow events held in San Diego, Tampa, Florida, and Toronto, Canada, volunteering at the Camp Widow gift store, and loved it. Purpose was everywhere. There's a certain giving you do when you're talking, just talking, to someone grieving, even if merely helping them select an item to purchase. You choose your words differently, your tone; you look at them with something different in your eyes. They may not sense it, but your heart is reaching out to theirs—and you can feel that blessed exchange between souls, part of our divine design. Some of my friends wondered why I had become a part of a secular organization, but their concern made little sense to me. Would Jesus say Christians only?

In the five years since the accident, I had hoped to meet someone who had had the same thing happen to them, the losing of a husband and son. Amazingly, and with some gratitude to God, no one who had attended any of the Camp Widow events fit the bill and experienced the exact same husband-and-son catastrophe. Of course that was good, but I continued to wait. If they were out there, my heart longed to come into their presence. Nothing else would suffice.

In the meantime, the next Camp Widow event was in Toronto. God had blessed me with the means to continue to follow the events to volunteer, and so, of course, I would be there.

I didn't know it but so too would be my emotional match.

- Debbie -

Toronto, Out of the Question

The bright light from my laptop filled my dark bedroom as I searched late into the night, feeling the need for more of what I knew to be the key to my survival—the company of others who would tend my wounds.

"Widow" in the search bar triggered a healthy list of bereavement support but only one caught my eye. The Camp Widow website offered weekends together and included pictures of beautiful locations with smiling people and even dancing. I knew I had to go. At that point, it had never crossed my mind that I would ever have fun again.

The next event would be in July in San Diego, only 90 minutes away from my house, but on the same block of days that I was taking the kids on a cruise—one that had been planned and on the schedule since before Jimbo and Nick died. We were now going to use it as a celebration of Jimbo and Nick, and the kids were looking forward to it. Moving it off our calendar was not an option, which came with some heartache for me—I really wanted, really *needed* to be in the presence of other grievers. The following Camp Widow event after July would be in September in Toronto. September was okay, but Toronto wasn't. I don't travel alone very well. I could venture away from home by myself an hour and a half down Interstate 5 to San Diego, but 2,500 miles to Toronto was not an option. I closed the book, and my laptop, on the idea. I'd go the following year to San Diego and hope to find a group or groups to help get me by in the meantime.

Rats. I really wanted to go.

But it turned out that I was not the final word on the subject. The Holy Spirit kept it alive, prompting me to go on a near-daily basis. "Go, Debbie, make the move. You have to go," He would say, over and over again to my spirit.

"Out of the question," I would reply. "Flying to another country by myself to meet people I don't know at this time in my life, in particular, is a non-starter from the get-go. I couldn't fathom going during good times, so how would going now make any sense?"

And yet, the prompts kept coming, a constant pulling on my heart. The Holy Spirit was unrelenting and undaunted by what seemed to be perfectly logical arguments why I should stay home. Finally, I could avoid it no longer. I went online and registered for Toronto, indicating I had lost a husband and a son in the same accident. "Lord, I hope you know what you are doing."

What a silly thing to say.

The moments in Toronto after arriving and getting settled into my hotel room, and before Michele, founder of Camp Widow, stepped just ahead of me as I was entering the hotel ballroom for the first Camp Widow event of the weekend, I was filled with mixed emotions and a cluelessness about what the next three days held. *I can't believe I'm here,* I kept thinking to myself. *I just can't believe I'm here.* I didn't know it, but it was a theme that, in a few moments, would repeat itself in a way I could never imagine.

"Can I help you?" Michele said, clearly in a rush.

"Hi, yeah, I'm here for—"

"Oh! Are you Debbie Siciliani?" she interrupted.

"Yes, I am."

"I'm Michele!"

I looked at her blankly.

"Michele, from Camp Widow!" she said.

"Oh, hi, Michele, I—"

"There's someone here I want you to meet!" she blurted out with her eyes like saucers. She grabbed me by the hand.

"Okay," I said. "Who?"

"Her name is Deb Rooney! She's had the exact same loss as you— husband and son, oldest son. Plane crash. Lost them both."

"Wait. What?" I replied like I wasn't sure what had just been said to me. I felt my pulse begin to race. "At the same time?"

"Same time. She's been waiting almost five years to meet someone like you."

I started to shake and felt my knees begin to shudder. "Waiting to meet me?"

"You're not going to believe this, but she lives in Yorba Linda, which I hear is close to you, right?" she said as I felt my knees touch the carpet. "And, Debbie, guess what? She's a believer, just like you!"

It was all too much. I trembled and felt my hands join my knees on the carpet. God brought me to Toronto to introduce me to a sister in the Lord who lives down the freeway and knows my journey inside and out? Could He really be that good? "She's down the hall at the gift store," Michele pointed. "Do you want to meet her?"

As I walked down the hotel hallway toward the gift shop and Deb Rooney, I walked on the most nervous legs imaginable. I turned the corner to where she would be. A lovely brown-haired woman, who was busy straightening books on a display table, saw me, and as our eyes met, she immediately recognized the unbalanced expression on my face and held out her arms. I walked forward, and as I did, she let me inside, right there, next to her heart. That is when God's provision swept over and enveloped me. "I can't believe I'm here" was all I could say as I pulled her as close as I could. "I just can't believe I'm here." God had given me Deb, and God had given Deb me—sisters forever knitted together by the same loss and God's love.

Somewhere in Upland, California, a woman I had never heard of just got her prayer answered.

When I posted on Facebook by the end of the weekend, I was flying so high I almost didn't recognize myself or what it felt like to be me. Not only had I met somebody who could share in my exact experience, but she lived just 20 minutes from me all the way back in Southern California. My world had just righted itself. And even as we gave each other our final hug before getting on our return flights, Deb Rooney invited me to dinner back home with a widow's group she socialized with, including a woman named Gina, someone she was sure I would like. For me, it would be kind of like having a bit of Camp Widow waiting for me at home.

Before the day arrived when I was to meet Deb Rooney and a few other widows at a restaurant, I got a text from Amie, the teacher from my kids' school. She said she was excited to hear I was going to meet her mother's best friend at the widow's dinner, Gina Pastore, the widow of Frank Pastore.

"Frank Pastore. Frank Pastore. Where have I heard that name?" I said to myself.

Suddenly—"FRANK PASTORE?!" I screamed. "Big Wave Dave's friend who he asked everyone to pray for?"

Part 6
The Purpose

- *Gina* -

Perhaps, had we thought about it, Debbie Siciliani and I should have met prior to the widows' dinner, to get out of the way all of the marveling that we were sure to do now that God had brought us three Southern California girls together via Toronto. Because, once Debbie and I saw each other, none of the other four widows in attendance that night stood a chance of breaking into our isn't-God-amazing embrace. We found ourselves locked in conversation, connecting so many dots, while Deb Rooney was the perfect hostess to the others. But once the evening was completed, it was clear that for the three of us, a miracle had occurred to put us all in one place at the same time. Now, we thought, we needed to meet again. If God had called us together the way it was clear He had, then it was incumbent on us to explore why He had gone through so much trouble.

Then it dawned on us—our families! We weren't the only victims of the accidents that took Frank, Bill, Patrick, Jimbo, and Nick away from us. All of our surviving children were suffering and could use the comfort of each other. And so, that is what we did. We planned to meet, along with our kids, Deb's in-laws, and Big Wave Dave in her backyard in Yorba Linda.

The day arrived when we would all gather together, and immediately we luxuriated in the presence of each other, each giving the other somewhere to distribute so much inner ache. We carried each other's load just by looking into the eyes of people like us. As we did, I could see through my own watery, blurry eyes that everyone's shoulders began to lift. Relief was in every smile, every hug, every tear.

- *Deb Rooney* -

While it might have seemed as though our families coming together was the reason for our miraculous meeting, something else began to reveal itself. Each of us, Debbie, Gina, and I, had a strong desire to take the stories of our pain, share them with the world, and trust that each contained some healing. It wasn't that we felt obligated to, but we had a burden for widows and widowers, people like us who were experiencing so much heart hurt. If our stories might help someone else not feel so alone, then we were champing at the bit to tell them. Each of us knew it was a unique desire to have in common. Not everyone feels that way. Many would rather just take their pain and be alone with it.

We looked at each other. Was something going on between us that God had great intention for and was ordaining? Was God knitting our hearts together for a greater purpose than ourselves? Were we about to embark on reaching others for Jesus with our own stories of grief? None of us could escape that we had been brought together in a profound way; there had to be a reason. This could be it. This had to be it.

Then Gina had something to say.

"When I was 13," she offered, "I laid in the grass in my backyard and prayed that I could marry Frank, who was just a friend of my brother's at the time—I barely knew him. When I stayed quiet and listened for God to answer my prayer, as a nun from school had suggested, I suddenly heard a voice. 'I will grant your prayer,' God said, 'but Frank is going to die young.'"

Our mouths fell open.

"I couldn't believe what I was hearing," Gina continued. "I was sure that God misunderstood my prayer request. I decided to ask again and do a better job of it. And so, that is what I did. God's answer was the same as it was before, only this time He asked, 'So, do you still want to marry Frank?'"

"What did you say?" Debbie and I quickly asked.

"I told God yes. Three years later, we eloped. About 38 years later, when Frank was 55, he died."

After gathering our jaws, we knew. If God had orchestrated Gina's life, then God, in allowing us to come into a friendship with such extreme purpose, had orchestrated our lives by the same event—way back in 1974 in a backyard in Upland. Suddenly, great truths about God seemed to fall into place. Ephesians 2:10 says, "For we are God's handiwork, created in Christ Jesus to do good works, which God prepared in advance for us to do."

In advance.

God had the answer to our problem, and a purpose for our problem, before we even had the problem. God is never reacting to a catastrophe; nothing catches Him off guard. God knew, and God knows. God's purpose and plan started before our existence. We are not alone. We are not hidden. We are a part of a plan.

"Jesus uses our trials to wean us from earth and woo us to heaven," Spurgeon said. It means our lives, even our catastrophes, and especially when God draws near during our pain, are orchestrated—that is the beautiful side of grief. It's knowing that all of it is a part of a loving plan and will be used to reach us and others. God is God over all trials, over all cataclysms. He had planned our coming together 40 years prior.

"Hey, would you like to come in and be guests on my new radio show?" Gina offered spryly, like she had just hit on the greatest idea in history. We all looked at each other with eyes wide open. "Sure!"

It was step one. God was on the move.

- *Debbie* -

I couldn't tell if Gina and Deb were nervous, but as for me, I was freaking out. The idea that I would be on a radio show, broadcast over the airwaves to all of Los Angeles and beyond, telling the story of Jimbo and Nick, the aftermath, and God's mercy in and through all of it, was more than I could wrap my head around.

We met at a Denny's in the city of Glendale and made our way over to the KKLA studios in one car—them talking and me hardly saying a word. It was a lot to take in.

As we rode up the elevator to the fifth floor, the nerves increased. *Radio? Me? Can I do this?* I wondered. But once we stepped out, it appeared God had a message waiting for me. The suite number on the studio door was 550. I screamed, scaring Gina and Deb to death. Both my men had favorite numbers based on their football jerseys: Jimbo, 55; Nick, 50. They wore them relentlessly.

They're with me, I thought. *Their spirits are in this place.*

When we walked into the studio, who should walk in to greet us but Gina's co-host for the broadcast as he was for all her shows: Big Wave Dave.

BIG WAVE DAVE?!

ARE YOU KIDDING ME?

After coming undone that I would be on the radio with Big Wave Dave, the man I had followed for years and prayed for as he led the masses to pray for Frank Pastore's healing, it was as clear as day that God was executing His will in my life—in all three of our lives. After a few minutes, we stepped up to our mics and did the show, which, even in the midst of the grief we all still felt, was a true joy. It became clearer with each passing minute that we were being called to a new phase in our lives—the reaching out to others with a message of hope, joy, and a God who is in total control. What I didn't know then was Big Wave Dave would join us in our ministry as we traveled and shared our stories.

When the show wrapped, the engineer called out, "Okay, show number 28—in the can!"

"Show 28?" I said as I felt my knees go weak. June 28 is the date Jimbo and Nick went to be with God.

Ribbon, like confetti from heaven, was falling everywhere.

Part 7
A Braided
Conversation

Newport Beach, California, January 18, 2022

GINA:
Did either of you feel like you were going crazy, or just going through the motions like a robot? I would ask myself, "Am I losing it?" I remember feeling like I was lost in a blur of sadness, and I felt so numb.

DEBBIE:
Totally. That was my whole thing. I was fighting for my sanity. I thought it was slipping away from me every second. Beyond falling into depression, it was like my brain was in a fog at all times, which added to the grief.

DEB:
Brain fog sounds sort of funny but it's a real thing. No wonder it's recommended not to make important decisions in the beginning. I had a lot of fog in my head, so I sure am glad that I took that advice. There were times when I would think I would hear Bill in the house. I'd be like, "Dear God, am I going crazy?"

DEBBIE:
That's why it's so important to be with other widows and widowers, so they can look you in your eyes and say, "This is so normal. You're not alone!"

DEB:
Totally agree.

GINA:
There were a couple of people who saw me suffering and told me to take antidepressants, so I talked to my therapist and asked her if I should. She said, "Well, do you want to grieve now or do you want to grieve later? Because you're not going to sidestep it. You have to go through this process in order to heal. It will come." The more you let

yourself feel the pain, and work on grieving, the better you will be. The emotions are so big, it's like a tidal wave crashing over you.

DEB:
In the end, you have to grieve fully.

DEBBIE:
I'm glad you mentioned that. What do you think it means to grieve fully? How do we know when we are grieving fully?

DEB:
Well, here's my answer: You have to go to all the places you don't want to go and surrender to it and the process. Let yourself feel everything.

DEBBIE:
You have to face the excruciating pain head-on. No one can do it for you.

GINA:
So true.

DEBBIE:
Yes. No doubt.

GINA:
You know, it's funny—or maybe not so funny when you think about it—but people think that, like in my case, I lost a husband, and in both of your cases you lost a husband and a son, and that's the story, but it's not the full story. There are so many things that change when you lose a loved one, so many losses.

DEBBIE:
You're talking about secondary loss?

GINA:
Yes.

DEB:
It's like the deaths are just the epicenter of loss. Death is the rock that hits

the water but the ripples keep moving outward—and that's all loss too.

DEBBIE:

I lost friendships—I mean, I didn't lose friendships—they're still my best friends. But our close bond was also shared with our husbands. And when all of a sudden I was no longer a couple, everything changed and the whole dynamic had to shift. Now they go on without me, and that hurts. With Nick, I lost so much more. He was only 16. I wasn't done raising him yet. All my hopes and dreams of him graduating from high school, then college, starting a family were now gone forever. It just goes on and on. I also lost the look in peoples' eyes that said they knew what to do with me, how to identify with me. As soon as I lost Jimbo and Nick, people were a little uncomfortable with how to treat me. But who can blame them, really? There's no guide book on how to treat grievers. So when God brought the three of us together, my best friends were utterly relieved.

GINA:

I loved being married to Frank. It's so weird to call myself a "widow."

DEBBIE:

Isn't it?

GINA:

I had no idea how much that meant to me and was a part of me and my identity until it was ripped away. I still wear my wedding ring. It's been almost a decade since Frank passed away, but he'll always be a part of me. He's ingrained in my soul, and yet I've learned to become whole again and have become a stronger person because of all I have experienced.

DEB:

You guys know how much I love my daughter-in-law, Erynn. Well, it was tough when a few years after the crash, there she was moving on and falling in love with a boy not Patrick and getting remarried and having a daughter and, of course, she has to—life moves on. But let me tell you, I had many conversations with my counselor about how to be at peace with that.

DEBBIE:
That's exactly how my mother-in-law felt about me. When I married Ron, she was happy for me and yet sad at the same time.

DEB:
It's very bittersweet.

GINA:
I was going to say, people may not know what to do with you, or how to react or behave, but then again, they really can't know, because they haven't experienced the loss.

DEBBIE:
I certainly don't hold it against anybody. Everybody is just trying their best.

GINA:
I remember this woman came up to me at Frank's memorial service and took me by the shoulders and said, "You're young and pretty. Don't worry." I was thinking, "What?" She was worried that I was wanting to remarry? Oh my goodness, that was the last thing on my mind.

DEB:
Ugh.

GINA:
As if to say, hey, you'll find a guy to replace Frank in no time. At the funeral, no less!

DEB ROONEY:
As if you're already thinking about moving on? You've got to be kidding!

GINA:
Trust me, the last thing on my mind was trying to replace my precious husband.

DEB:
But it was a little worse than that, right?

GINA:

It was an awful feeling, yes. But hey, in the moment she thought she was delivering the most wonderful piece of news imaginable, God bless her. Until I went through my loss, I'm sure I didn't know what to say to people either. We all want to have these magic words that make other's feel better instantly.

DEBBIE:

Isn't it the truth! I think we should help people know that when you experience a devastating loss, it is perfectly appropriate to tell your loved ones, "You don't need to say anything. Feel free to say nothing at all."

GINA:

Especially when they use Scripture, or platitudes.

DEB:

Oh, the people who love to quote Scripture!

GINA:

Here's the problem with using Scripture or platitudes: you are in such a place of deep personal pain, it's like you've been hit with an avalanche, and under 10 feet of snow, and then someone walks up and hands you a spoon. The pain is just too enormous. Really, it's better if they just saying nothing, nothing at all.

DEBBIE:

True. Save the spoons.

DEB:

I had some friends who would just drop by and say, "Let's go shopping" or "Let's take a ride." And then they would just let me cry—and that was okay. I appreciated just being with them.

DEBBIE:

My best friends and family spent hour after hour just sitting with me and letting me talk. And cry. And scream. They even cried with me.

GINA:

You know in the book of Job, every time his friends opened their mouths, that's when things went wrong.

DEB:

Then there are those who think that if they bring up Bill's or Patrick's name and I cry, then they've done something wrong. I like thinking about Bill and Patrick and I like that they remember them too.

DEBBIE:

That's how I felt. I liked when people talked about Nick and Jimbo; I wanted their names said as much as could be. I remember having this fear that people would forget them.

GINA:

So I think we can all agree. It's wonderful for others to talk about our loved ones who have passed. Just don't give advice.

DEBBIE:

Or helpful quotes.

DEB:

Or think you'll be comforted by their words, or somehow fixed.

GINA:

That will come.

DEB:

In time.

GINA:

Lots of time.

DEB:

In the beginning it feels like you're living in a bad dream and can't wake up. But God uses this time to draw you closer and make you more dependent on Him. We find ourselves clinging to Him for survival.

GINA:

It is every person's fear, losing a spouse or child. Going through grief is the most difficult journey you'll ever experience, and yet I can honestly say, I've never felt more connected to the Lord. I relied on Him daily for my comfort and strength. Still do.

DEBBIE:

A beautiful friend once said to me, it's like all of us Christians are in a big circle, but then there's an inner circle where all the grievers are on their knees holding onto the feet of Jesus. The feeling of God's presence is so strong because He is so close to the brokenhearted. No one wants to be there, but they are the joyous ones.

GINA:

And yet, what we would do to have our loved one's back. It's a very strange thing.

DEBBIE:

Yup. I mean, ask the person filled with joy if they'd like to have their loved one back and they'd be like, "Without a doubt." Ask Joni Eareckson Tada if she would like to walk again; my guess is that she would be very tempted, even though her quadriplegia has brought God so close.

DEB:

And given her such great purpose.

GINA:

Having purpose is such a gift! We all need a reason to get up in the morning, a reason to live and thrive.

DEB:

God promises to provide for those who grieve a crown of beauty instead of ashes, the oil of joy instead of mourning, and a garment of praise instead of a spirit of despair. They will be called oaks of righteousness, a planting of the LORD for the display of His splendor.

DEBBIE:

So beautiful.

GINA:
Honestly, I never dreamed I'd be ministering to so many going through loss and pain. I never planned on any of this. Through my darkest hours, God has enabled me to encourage others, and that feels so good. As I look in the rear-view mirror, I see God's plan for my life, His purpose and provision.

DEB:
It's amazing, the beautiful side of grief is three-pronged. Number one: joy follows suffering. Number two: suffering brings purpose, and purpose is meaning, and meaning is beautiful. And three: God had your joy and healing in mind before you were even born—before the world began. God's Word says that He has made everything beautiful in its time. And that eternity has been set in the human heart: "Yet no one can fathom what God has done from beginning to end."

DEBBIE:
A mystery from beginning to end.

GINA:
A braided cord of three—like us.

DEBBIE:
Amen to that. Amen to all of it.

Ref: Psalm 34:18; Isaiah 61:3; Ecclesiastes 3:11

A rope made of three cords is hard to break.
-Ecclesiastes 4:12, GNT

Postscript

DEBBIE:

People are always really amazed when I tell them that Gail, one of my three dearest friends who drew even closer to me during the dark days after Jimbo and Nick died, moved to Idaho with her husband and ended up renting a house next door to a lovely couple with the last name, *Rooney*. They hit it off nicely and it prompted a phone call from Gail to me. "Debbie, this is a stretch, but is there any chance that your friend Deb Rooney has a son named Colin?"

"Yes, she does."

"He's married, right?"

"Yes."

"Where do they live?"

"Somewhere in Idaho. I have no idea where."

"Well, let me ask you this. Is his wife pregnant?"

"Yes."

"Debbie, you are not going to believe this!"

It is amazing how vines from this story continue to intertwine and bring us closer together. To think that these two major characters in the story of our lives should move next door to each other—all the way in Idaho—is mind-boggling.

But it is just the beginning.

After God brought Gina, Deb, and me together, Gina would give us frequent updates on another family crisis: Delia, the mother-in-law of her daughter, Christina, was battling cancer. Of course we prayed, keeping in mind the fear that both Delia and her husband, Ron, were going through. How well we knew those awful moments.

After Delia passed, I kept up my vigil praying for the agony Ron must have been experiencing in the emptiness of their house. The fact that I once was there for Christina's daughter's second birthday brought it home all the more. I never did meet Ron but it helped me put a picture with the pain.

For some reason, a few years later, it was me who came to mind when Christina, hoping to tend to her father-in-law's loneliness, wondered who might be a fun coffee companion. When she messaged me on Facebook, it was such a shock. "Me? Out of all the people you could think of, you reached out to me?"

But it did make some sense—we both had lost a spouse, we both had named a son Nick, and, come to find out, we both lost mothers by the time we were six. That is probably why the first time we met for coffee, our conversation lasted nine hours. That and the fact that God appears to like tying up loose ends.

Fourteen months later, Ron and I married. Today, Gina and I are friends, but we are also family. I am the stepmother-in-law to Gina's daughter. My post-catastrophe life, and Gina's, and Deb's too, continue to have the fingerprints of God all over it.

Acknowledgments

To our co-writer Dave Franco, we appreciate your thoughtful guidance in bringing three journeys together into one heartfelt story. Thank you for making this such a wonderful process, and may your masterful, insightful writing style continue to bless many.

To all our beloved friends who helped us through our season of grief, and still remain in our lives today. We are extremely thankful for all the love and support you offered us. Thank you for your steadfast friendships.

To our extended families who gave us endless support, not only to each of us, but our children. We are forever grateful.

To Jay Jaso, I am so thankful for you! You have brought me a newness of life and renewed love that I never thought possible. I love you. –Debi Rooney Jaso.

To Ron Smallwood, I am so grateful for you! Thank you for allowing me to honor my past with Jimbo and Nick, and yet partner me in a loving marriage again. We will see Jimbo and your Delia once again someday. I love you. –Debbie Siciliani Smallwood.

To our children, we love each and every one of you beyond what words can say. Frank and Jessica, Erynn and Adam, Sean and Jana, Christina and Josh, Colin and Jessica, Chelsie, Greg, and Sammy, you have each allowed your lives to be enhanced by the losses, and the legacy each of you demonstrates blows our minds.

To Bill and Patrick, Jimbo and Nick, and Frank, we miss you

endlessly, but look forward to our reunion with you in Heaven. We carry you in our hearts forever, and the impact you have made on our lives is immeasurable.

To our Lord and Savior, we have no words to thank You enough for Your sacrifice on Calvary. You defeated death. You bring new life and You offer us continual hope. Because of You, we will see our loved ones once again. We offer this story to You.

About the Authors

Gina Pastore became tragically widowed when her husband, Frank, was struck down on his motorcycle after leaving the studio from doing his weekly radio broadcast on KKLA's The Frank Pastore Show. Gina is the radio host of Real Life with Gina Pastore & David James, author of Picking Up My Shattered Pieces, and an inspirational speaker. She has two adult children, Frank and Christina, and five grandchildren.

Debi Rooney Jaso is an inspirational speaker and special contributor on Real Life radio program. Debi experienced a heart-breaking loss when both her husband and eldest son were killed in a plane crash. Today, she encourages others to live steadfast in Christ through pain and loss. Debi has two adult sons, Sean and Colin, and one son in heaven, Patrick. She is happily remarried to Jay Jaso, father to two adult children, and together they share ten grandchildren.

Debbie Siciliani-Smallwood is an inspirational speaker and special contributor on Real Life radio program. Debbie experienced a horrific loss when both her husband and eldest son died in a car accident. Today, she motivates others to walk boldly through life's "curve balls." Debbie has three children, Greg, Chelsie, and Sammy, and one son in heaven, Nick. She is happily remarried to Ron Smallwood, father to two married sons, and together they enjoy three grandchildren.

Dave Franco is a former New York City ad copywriter who, after 25 years of writing campaigns, was asked to write a book for a client, an event that has led to 14 public and private-use books over the last 11 years, plus scores of magazine and website features. He continues to ghostwrite as well as speak on the power of story.

If you would like to contact Gina, Deb, or Debbie about speaking or other engagements, please email **beautifulsideofgrief@gmail.com**.